THE CHRISTIAN
IMPERATIVE

THE
CHRISTIAN
IMPERATIVE

Being
The Kellogg Lectures
at The Episcopal Theological School,
Cambridge, Massachusetts
February 1955

MAX WARREN

1 9 5 5
CHARLES SCRIBNER'S SONS
NEW YORK

TO
George Cooper
Madge Lea
AND
Ella Jennings
UPON WHOSE FRIENDSHIP
AND FORBEARANCE I HAVE
DEPENDED FOR SO LONG

Contents

Preface

Our generation has been characterized by a vast expansion of the frontiers of human thought at a time when facilities for travel, not to mention other methods of communication, have become such that, for an increasing number of people of all races, the world is contracting into a neighbourhood. A revolution in perspective is involved and the adjustment to this new perspective is not the least part of the travail of our times.

This sudden 'expansion' and 'contraction,' in turn, poses a new range of questions for the Christian who is concerned with the Christian Mission in the world, and challenges many traditional assumptions. Meanwhile this revolution in perspective is itself compounded of great economic, political and social changes. It is no wonder that for many Christians there is a profound confusion of mind as to the very basis of the Christian Mission itself. The challenge of vocation is for many to-day no clear-cut, if costly, matter of response to some undisputed demand. More often than not it has become a 'problem' to which no solution can be offered which stands out as unquestionably right.

There is, then, a need to investigate afresh the basis of the Christian Mission, to reaffirm the fundamentals of Christian obedience and then to try to re-interpret both the basis and the fundamentals in terms relevant to the situation which confronts us today.

This investigation will involve the best efforts of many, both by way of a rediscovery of the nature of those imperatives which govern Christian discipleship and of a new appraisal of the task committed to us. In the process the words 'Mission' and 'Missionary' will need to come under review in order that the Christian Mission may be seen within the new perspective of our time.

To such an investigation the chapters which follow are a small contribution. They consist, with a few verbal changes, of a series of lectures given in the United States in February 1955. The 'lecture' form has been retained, as being more personal and more direct. The occasion of these lectures was a visit to the Episcopal Theological School at Cambridge, Massachusetts. An annual lectureship in memory of his father, Frederic Rogers Kellogg, had been established in 1953 by the Rev. Frederic Brainerd Kellogg. It was my privilege to be able to accept the invitation from the Dean and Faculty of the School to give these 'Kellogg' lectures for 1955. To Dean Taylor, the Members of the Faculty, the Alumni and the students of the school who endured, with such patient courtesy, the 'marathon' of listening to five lectures in twenty-four hours, I would pay the tribute of my astonishment and gratitude.

One other duty of acknowledgment must be paid. In the Revised Standard Version for I Samuel 30. 24

we read 'For as his share is who goes down into the battle, so shall his share be who stays by the baggage.' That that promise will be redeemed in the realm where true judgments of value reside I have no doubt. Meanwhile, it does not often look like it in this world. I am the more glad, therefore, to have the opportunity of dedicating this book to three of my friends and colleagues whose fidelity in looking after 'the baggage' has been as good an illustration of obedience to the Christian imperative as any I know.

M. A. C. W.

NOTE:

The renderings of New Testament passages are normally those of the American Revised Standard Version of the Bible, copyrighted 1946 and 1952 by permission of Thomas Nelson and Sons Ltd., Edinburgh, and, in U.S.A., of the Division of Christian Education of the National Council of Churches.

INTRODUCTION

THE Christian imperative is a compulsion born of a discovery. This discovery is recorded in the New Testament under three aspects, calculated between them to challenge the most varied temperaments. In St. John 3. 16 we find—'God so loved the world that he gave his only Son, that whoever believes in him should not perish but have eternal life.' There is a range and a depth in that revelation which embraces every man from the most hopeful to the most hopeless. In Ephesians 5. 25 we find—'Christ loved the church and gave himself up for her.' In those words we are reminded that God's love took a particular historical form. History becomes meaningful, the locale is illuminated, community is consecrated. Oneness with God means oneness with our fellow-men. And then in Galatians 2. 20 we find—'The Son of God, who loved me and gave himself for me.' The individual discovers that he is not a spectator of history but a significant part of it, not the average everyman but someone unique.

> *I come in the little things,*
> *Saith the Lord:*
> *My starry wings*
> *I do forsake,*
> *Love's highway of humility to take:*
> *Meekly I fit my stature to your need.*

In beggar's art
About your gates I shall not cease to plead—
As man, to speak with man—
Till by such art
I shall achieve My Immemorial Plan,
Pass the low lintel of the human heart.[1]

For some the immense range and depth of the love of God is compulsive, if for no other reason than that it alone can embrace the manifold wonders and perplexities of life as we know it. For others, the very fascination of the historical process, the fears and hopes of men outworking in the movements of our day, clamour for a revelation that can be seen to be relevant. For yet others, tortured by a self-knowledge which is incomplete, the miracle is to find One 'unto whom all hearts be open, all desires known, and from whom no secrets are hid', and who can love us in spite of all that understanding. For all in their several ways there comes the moment in which they become fully aware of the divine compulsion: each in his own way says, 'The love of Christ controls',[2] and seeks the grace to live so controlled.

Here it is then, in the discovery of the love of God, that we are to recognize the true source of the Christian imperative. Here is the only dynamic for endurance; for it is only love that 'bears all things, believes all things, hopes all things, endures all things';[3] and

[1] *Immanence*, by Evelyn Underhill (*Oxford Book of English Mystical Verse*, 1924, pp. 524–525).
[2] II Cor. 5. 14.
[3] I Cor. 13. 7.

love of that quality is God Himself by His Holy Spirit making the things of Jesus come alive in us.

It is with that understanding that I have tried to present the Christian imperative as it has to be obeyed in different ways in the Christian Mission of our day. For my main divisions I have taken the divine commission as recorded in the Gospels, from which we can distinguish the following commands—'Go preach', 'Go teach', 'Go heal' and 'Go baptize'. Something of the peculiar difficulty of our obedience in the world of our own day I have attempted to describe in Chapter V under the title, 'The "how" of obedience'.

1

Go Preach

YOU will remember how, in his letter to the
Christians at Rome, Paul gives passionate expression to his love and hope for his own people, the
ancient Israel of God. To me it always seems that
chapters nine to eleven of that letter, in which this
emotion is laid bare, are more in the nature of a
soliloquy than part of an argument. There we over-
hear Paul wrestling in his own mind with some of
the profoundest religious problems of all. Divine
predestination and human freedom, the righteousness
of God, revelation and the validity of its prophetic
interpretation, the meaning of history, the nature of
hope, all are here 'focussed to a pin-point's burning
intensity'. But Paul is wrestling in no private mental
gymnasium of his own. Like Jacob he wrestles with
God. Almost we can hear him challenging his destiny,
striving with God against the divine decree that he,
'an Hebrew of the Hebrews', should have had committed to him the Mission to the Gentiles, when all
his natural disposition and apparent qualifications
marked him out as an apostle to his own people.

Some such imaginative understanding of the context is, I believe, called for if we are going to appreciate the great appeal for missionaries which comes in Romans Chapter 10, verse 11 which begins—

'The Scripture says, "No one who believes in him will be put to shame". For there is no distinction between Jew and Greek; the same Lord is Lord of all and bestows his riches upon all who call upon him. For, "every one who calls upon the name of the Lord will be saved".'

So he leads up to his appeal—

'But how are men to call upon him in whom they have not believed? And how are they to believe in him of whom they have never heard? And how are they to hear without a preacher?'

Must we not read into those words something of the challenge to responsibility which Paul expresses for himself when he cries out 'Woe to me if I do not preach the gospel.'[1]

Before we go on to consider the bearing of all this on the Christian Mission to-day, what is the meaning for us of obedience to the command 'go preach', what is to be the content of our preaching, it may help to consider with some care the New Testament words which describe this ministry. There are six words used in the New Testament, each of which is translated in English by the word 'preach'. While we shall be wise not to press too far the different nuances of meaning suggested by the Greek, yet they do serve in some measure to indicate the range and scope of what is

[1] I Cor. 9. 16.

compassed by the word 'preach' and therefore what is involved in our imperative.

The *first*, a very common word *laleō*, may denote no more than making oneself heard. We, who can sometimes hardly hear ourselves think for the confused murmur of the world's debate all around us, will not be inclined to despise this elementary meaning. A preacher must make himself heard. Even this simple word has, however, a primary meaning, 'to utter oneself'. To minds already disposed to think of the Word of God as being His self-utterance this article of speech proved congenial. We can understand the frequency of its use in Scripture to denote those utterances by which God communicated His mind and will either directly or through His messengers. It is interesting to find it used of that scene described in St. Mark 2. 2 where we read—

> 'And many were gathered together, so that there was no longer room for them, not even about the door; and he was preaching (*laleō*) the word to them.'

In that simple incident we can see the Preacher having to make Himself heard, speaking the words of God, Himself the uttered Word of God.

Another term, used rarely in the New Testament, the word *dia͠ggellō* has its own importance because it suggests a penetration of purpose and a sense of urgency. It means to announce everywhere, to carry a message right throughout a whole area. The context of its only use in the Gospels is a solemn one. Jesus is on His last journey up to Jerusalem. His face is steadfastly set towards all that lies before Him. Something

of the purposeful mien of Jesus must have communicated itself, a sense of great events impending. One
and another wanting to be 'in on things' came forward
to join his company. But they did not understand.
They lacked any sense of urgency. It is to all such men
who offer such a discipleship that Jesus says now as
He said then, 'Leave the dead to bury their own dead;
but as for you, go and proclaim (*diaggellō*) the Kingdom
of God.'[1]

Associated with this word, and used more fre-
quently, though not in the Gospels, is that other com-
pound verb, *kataggellō*. Its usage seems to hint at
something of what we understand by the word 'advertisement'. To Athenians in their scepticism Paul ad-
vertises Christ—'What therefore you worship as unknown, this I proclaim (*kataggellō*) to you' (Acts
17. 23). In another passage there is a peculiar pathos
in the use of the word. Paul is writing to the Philippians and describing some of the difficulties of his
ministry as a prisoner. Caged, he has to watch others
flying free. Using a word of great significance which
we will consider in a moment, he sees all of these
preachers as, in some sense, heralds of the gospel—
'Some indeed', he writes, 'preach Christ from envy and
rivalry, but others of good will.' Then he finds himself
forced to distinguish further. 'The latter do it out of
love, knowing that I am put here for the defence of
the gospel; the former *advertise* (*kataggellō*) Christ
out of partisanship.' Is there perhaps a hint at their
self-advertisement? It is, at least, suggested by the

[1] Luke 9. 60

words 'not sincerely'. But by grace Paul triumphs over his bitterness, and with a sense of humour laughs his way to gladness because, after all, 'whether in pretense or in truth Christ is *advertised* (*kataggellō*); and in that I rejoice'.[1]

We need not dwell long over the *fourth* term *dialegomai*. We read in Acts 18. 4 that Paul 'argued (*dialegomai*) in the synagogue every sabbath and persuaded Jews and Greeks'. Again in Acts 19. 8 we hear of him in Ephesus 'arguing and pleading about the kingdom of God'. The word suggests the approach of the apologist, who mingles thought with thought. We hear Paul before Felix as 'he argued (*dialegomai*) about justice and self-control and future judgment' (Acts 24. 25). We must never underestimate the importance of this aspect of our preaching, though we do well to bear in mind that argument can have a soporific effect in more senses than one. You will recollect how at Troas 'a young man named Eutychus was sitting in the window. He sank into a deep sleep', we are told, 'as Paul talked still longer (*dialegomai*); and being overcome by sleep, he fell down from the third story and was taken up dead' (Acts 20. 9). It is recorded of the great Charles Simeon that, preaching in Holy Trinity Church, Cambridge, on one occasion, he had been arguing the gospel for some sixty minutes. Perceiving that a large part of the congregation was asleep he woke them and then started again. Simeon was, undisputedly, one of the greatest preachers of the gospel, but I suggest to you that, as a method,

[1] Phil. 1. 15–18.

that indicated by the word *dialegomai* has its limitations!

The *fifth* term to denote *preaching* is that great word *kērussō*, used by Paul himself in our passage from Romans (10. 14), 'How are they to hear without *someone acting as a herald.*' Here surely is an echo of the word of our Lord, preserved in some, though not in all, manuscripts of St. Mark 16. 15—'Go into all the world and preach (*kērussō*) the gospel to the whole creation.' Certainly that same gospel affords Paul all the necessary warrant for his use of the word. Do we not read in St. Mark 1. 38 the words of Jesus 'Let us go on to the next towns, that I may preach there also (*kērussō*).'? Again how unforgettable must have been the charge given to the twelve on the mountain, when Jesus 'called to him those whom he desired; and they came to him. And he appointed twelve, to be with him, and to be sent out to preach (*kērussō*).'[1] And we will not forget the man delivered from the haunting of demons, who being expressly sent home by Jesus to bear witness to what had happened to him, 'went away and began to proclaim (*kērussō*) . . . how much Jesus had done for him'.[2]

This word 'to herald' is a word of great dignity. The man who acts as a herald brings advance tidings of someone coming, someone actually at hand, of the imminence of a great event. What is more the herald speaks with authority. And I suggest to you that one part of this authority lies not so much in the *office* of the herald as in the fact that he is *in the secret* of what

[1] Mark 3. 13-14. [2] Mark 5. 20.

is about to happen, he knows who is coming. The herald of the New Testament is the prophet of the Old Testament. To him also are committed the oracles of God.[1] Calling people back to recognize what God has done, appealing to them to respond to what He is doing now, they are fearless in their insistence of His consistency, and so they speak of what they know He is going to do—'Surely the Lord does nothing without revealing his secret to his servants the prophets.'[2]

I have kept to the end the greatest word of all, the word which defines the preacher as one who brings glad tidings—*euaggelidzō*. While shepherds watched their flocks by night they heard the good news of a Saviour. The angel brought glad tidings of great joy (*euaggelidzō*). The message which Jesus Himself heralded (*kērussō*) was the good news (*euaggelion*) of the reign of God,[3] from which our words 'evangel' and 'evangelist' derive. To his own forerunner, perplexed by the unfolding ministry of Jesus, the message was sent, 'Tell John what you have seen and heard: the blind receive their sight, the lame walk, lepers are cleansed, and the deaf hear, the dead are raised up, the poor have good news preached to them (*euaggelidzō*)'[4]—thus the prophets have been fulfilled. And later on, looking back on His ministry, Jesus can say to the contentious Pharisees, 'the Law and the prophets were until John; since then the good news of the kingdom of God is preached' (*euaggellidzō*).[5] In the

[1] Rom. 3. 2; I Peter 4. 11.   [2] Amos 3. 7.
[3] Mark 1. 14–15.   [4] Luke 7. 22.
[5] Luke 16. 16.

same Gospel (St. Luke 9) after we have read that the disciples had been sent out to be heralds (*kērussō*, v. 2) we see them going through the villages 'preaching the gospel (*euaggelidzō*), and healing everywhere'. It is the same gospel to which Paul testifies in writing to the Corinthians when, in preparing to recapitulate his essential message, he says by way of preface, 'I would remind you, brethren, in what terms I preached to you the gospel (*euaggelidzō*), which you received, in which you stand, by which you are saved, if you hold it fast.'[1]

This good news of the Gospel, this record of what God has done, is doing and is going to do, is the essential theme of the Christian preacher. In the second Epistle to Timothy we read the solemn charge, 'preach the word, be urgent in season and out of season. . .'.[2] There is an old paraphrase of that verse which runs, 'Thou art a Minister of the Word: mind thy business.' With that exhortation let us turn to consider in greater detail the nature of this assignment, what premises should be our foundation, and what are the contemporary problems by which we shall be confronted.

Our first reaction to a task so all-embracing and so properly awe-inspiring, in which we are called to be 'the aroma of Christ to God among those who are being saved and among those who are perishing, to one a fragrance from death to death, to the other a

---

[1] I Cor. 15. 1–2.   [2] II Tim. 4. 2.
[3] II Cor. 2. 15–16.

fragrance from life to life', is to say with Paul, 'Who is sufficient for these things?'[3]

Paul was surely conscious of this hesitation both for himself and for all who feel, together with the compulsion of the gospel, a shrinking at their own manifest incapacity. In that passage in Romans 10 with which we began, the final query of the Apostle is 'how can men preach unless they are sent?' So here in this letter to the Corinthians Paul draws strength for himself and his hearers from a deep assurance which can say in all humility 'we are not . . . peddlers of God's word; but as men of sincerity, as commissioned by God, in the sight of God we speak in Christ'.[1] Our imperative is no philosopher's deduction from the moral order. It is the Word of God spoken to us in Christ at the point where we accepted from His hands ordination to our ministry.

We speak 'in Christ' and our speech is addressed to men and women. That is the implicit, even when it is not the explicit, assumption of the various Greek words which, we have seen, are translated in English by the word 'preach'. We evangelize men and women, *not* situations, *not* humanity, *not* abstractions of any kind but only 'flesh and blood'. This is a point of real importance and I think that if we keep it clear we shall be saved from a good deal of confusion in our thought about preaching. There is a presentation of the gospel which can properly be addressed to situations, to the relationships between men and women

[1] II Cor. 2. 17.

which create situations. Preaching may have a part to play in reaching these men and women but the effect of preaching on the situation is a by-product, not the object of the preaching. We will see later how some of our other imperatives bear more directly on situations. Let us keep the word 'preach' to a direct activity between preacher and hearer.

To evangelize is to proclaim good news to men in such a way as to elicit the response of acceptance. To evangelize is more than prophecy. It is even more than preaching the gospel. It is preaching the gospel *with effect*, with signs following. You will remember the definition which runs—

> 'To evangelize is so to present Christ Jesus, in the power of the Holy Spirit, that men may come to put their trust in Him as Saviour and follow Him as Lord in the fellowship of His Church.'

We shall, I think, be on firm ground if we hold to that definition and confine the evangelistic aspect of preaching to what does, in fact, lead men and women to conversion and church membership. This is not to deny that there is an important place for the giving of a testimony, although it is not heeded, to witnessing even though our witness is rejected. We have our Lord's own command to do these very things. But I would suggest that if, evangelistically, our preaching is to have a cutting edge it should be seen as preaching 'with signs following'.

If, then, we are clear that our objective is men and women let us approach them through preaching with a due awareness of the prevenient grace of God. To dwell on this prevenience will do more to keep us humble and hopeful than any other exercise. For to dwell on the fact that before ever we preach, God has been at work in those to whom we preach, is to get ourselves in proportion. To realize further that, in so far as our speech is effective, it is that we are speaking 'in Christ', that the divine initiative is at work through us, is to be saved from any inflation due to an estimate of our own success, or any deflation leading to the sin of despair through the calculation of our own failure.

We can discern the divine initiative in three truths about the men and women to whom we preach.

The *first* truth is that *God made them.* That is the deepest truth about any man or woman whom we seek to evangelize. Heredity did not make them; environment did not make them: education did not make them: God made them. We need to be seized of that tremendous affirmation if we are to be set free from the paralyzing determinism of so much modern thinking.

Note that I have not said that heredity has no influence, that environment does not matter, that education is without significance. All I have sought to insist is that the primary significance of any man or woman for the Christian is that they are, to use a striking rendering of I Corinthians 3. 9, 'God's field',[1] are of the very stuff of the divine initiative when 'in the beginning God created the heavens and the earth'.[2]

It makes a vast difference if, as we approach our fellows we see in them the 'image' of God, however

[1] Revised Standard Version.   [2] Gen. 1. 1.

defaced, and see that first of all as being evidence of the divine initiative. If we genuinely approach men and women like that we shall start with a great hope. For however deeply conditioned they may be by heredity and environment and education, the primary condition of their existence is that God made them.

May I add this thought that if we so behold them we shall be more likely to follow the example of Moses when, seeing a bush on fire and yet unconsumed, he turned aside to see and discovered God, and found himself on holy ground. If we take the divine initiative seriously then evangelism becomes one approach to the Holy. Let me be very bold and press this illustration of the burning bush beyond its legitimate meaning, but not beyond a legitimate inference from the initiative of God, and say that in our evangelism we shall often come upon men and women who are on fire with lust, aflame with ambition, burning with cruelty, 'yet they are not consumed'. In the very midst of the fire is one like unto the Son of God. Here is holy ground, when at first sight we thought we were in hell. *But*, 'if I go down into hell, thou art there also', as the Book of Common Prayer version of Psalm 139. 8 reminds us.

I am convinced that a belief in the divine initiative in creation—in all created life—is a vital theological assumption for the evangelist if he is to prove himself in his 'work of faith and labor of love and steadfastness of hope in our Lord Jesus Christ'.[1]

[1] I Thess. 1. 3.

[25]

The *second* truth about the men and women to whom we preach is that *they stand in history, and that God is in control of that history.* Having insisted that the prior significance for man is that God made him and *not* heredity or environment or education, we must go on to see what is the significance for man of precisely these things which, summed up, are history.

The men and women we seek to evangelize stand in a particular history as well as within universal history. Our task is to evangelize them where they stand. Their actual place of standing matters, for they have responsibilities there and God has responsibilities there. I would suggest to you that the underlying significance of Abraham in the biblical revelation lies in the fact that he is immensely significant for history. He inaugurates the history of the chosen people. He is the prototype of the man of faith. As the inaugurator of the history of the chosen people, he is the archetypal *man of responsibility.* As the man of faith-obedience he proclaims that God has an active concern with the course of events which we call history. In and through Abraham, God is revealed as accepting responsibility for history.

Thus heredity, environment, and education come into their own because the divine initiative is seen to be at work in all of them. God is working out a mighty pattern into which the strands of life and circumstance are woven. We who preach to men and women do not believe that life is determined by 'accidents'. We recognize the complicated inter-relationship of a multitude of factors for which God accepts responsibility and which depend ultimately upon His initiative. It is this conviction which lies behind the confidence with which Paul can say, 'We know that in everything God works for good with those who love him.'[1] It is our privilege as the lovers of God and His evangelists to bring within the embrace of that verse all those to whom we go with the gospel. Later I shall, I hope, show how this can be done as we study the other imperatives under which we stand.

The *third* fact about man, the man we seek to evangelize, is that *he stands in a particular relationship to God by virtue of his creation and his standing in history.* The whole purport of our preaching must be to see that the relationship is a *right* relationship.

Still thinking in terms of the divine initiative our key text must be, 'God was in Christ reconciling the world to himself.'[2] Concealed within that tremendous assertion is the truth that man needs to be reconciled. Man the creature has refused to co-operate with God his Creator. Man is in rebellion, is out of fellowship with God. What gives to man's history its dramatic quality, its real meaning, is that God refuses to allow man to perish in his rebellion, but seeks continuously to affirm the divinely intended fellowship by bringing man back into a right relationship with Himself. That in Christ we see not only the supreme example of self-sacrifice, not only humanity raised to its most sublime in self-surrender, not only the perfect Man, but God

[1] Rom. 8. 28.
[2] II Cor. 5. 19.

[27]

Himself at work, is the good news of the divine initiative.

The immediate relevance of this to the preacher himself is to be discovered in two texts from Paul's letter to the Christians of Galatia:

'When the time had fully come, God sent forth his Son.'[1]
'He who had set me apart before I was born, and had called me through his grace, was pleased to reveal his Son to me.[2]

Those two truths are for Paul the evangelist the two fundamental premises upon which his preaching of the gospel and indeed his whole life were built. The initiative at all times is with God. In evangelism we know that initiative as the power of the Holy Spirit. On this rock of confidence, assured of a grace sufficient for all our need, we can build our preaching ministry.

In our study we are now in a position from which to go forward to consider the principles which should govern our approach to our fellow-men. The communication of the Word, let us be clear from the outset, is a two-way process. It involves expression and reception. Unless what has been expressed has been received in the sense of being understood (and then either accepted or rejected) there has been, in fact, no communication. Need I add that from the point of view of the preacher there has been no evangelism? You possess a radiogram. There may be a man with a great message on the air at the very moment. But unless you and he are on the same wavelength there

[1] Gal. 4. 4.   [2] Gal. 1. 15–16.

has been, as far as he and you are concerned, no communication. We who preach need to remember that 'wave-length' matters. We have a most solemn responsibility before God to communicate the gospel. That means that we are called to wrestle with the problems of communication.

Our primary approach, our angle of vision, is governed by the fact that we must seek to see men as God sees them. Indeed when Paul says in the passage already quoted 'as commissioned by God, in the sight of God we speak in Christ',[1] he is really saying just that. The place of prayer in evangelism is the symbol of our awareness of this truth. We go out from His presence into His world taking that presence with us—'We are ambassadors for Christ, God making his appeal through us. We beseech you on behalf of Christ, be reconciled to God.'[2] We are, indeed, men 'entrusted with the message of reconciliation'.[3]

Within this angle of vision we can distinguish between the transcendent and the immanent approach of God Himself which must find its expression in our ministry. As transcendent, God speaks direct to man as a spiritual being. The directness is not affected by the medium of communication. What the preacher communicates is not his word but *the* Word. Our inescapable responsibility is to lift up Jesus Christ and Him crucified-risen. It is the work of the Holy Spirit to bring that 'lifting up' to the point of 'drawing men' into a right relationship with God. And in order

[1] II. Cor. 2. 17.   [2] II Cor. 5. 20.
[3] II Cor. 5. 19.

that we may be safeguarded from falsifying our perspective, failing to see men as God sees them, we are committed to the revelation set forth in Holy Scripture—'Whatsoever is not read therein, nor may be proved thereby, is not to be . . . thought requisite or necessary to salvation.'[1] 'Christ in all the Scriptures', as Luther has it, is our theme. Preaching which does not hold up Jesus, and in which that upholding is not based on Scripture, is not the preaching of the gospel, and it can hardly be the vehicle of the transcendent approach of God to men. The problems thereby raised for communication are, as we shall see, formidable.

Still within the angle of vision which seeks to see men as God sees them is the immanent approach from God to man. This is the way of *incarnation* whereby the life of the Church and the life of the Christian penetrate into the life of men in the world so that the Word of God is encountered at unexpected levels and in the midst of daily experience which is familiar.

This way of immanence is made effective in preaching by the deliberate activity of imagination, behind which must lie an effort, individual on the part of the preacher, or corporate on the part of the Church, to discover what life in the world really is for the men who live there. In his first letter to the Corinthians Paul shows us what lay behind his preaching. He wrote

'Though I am free from all men, I have made myself a slave to all, that I might win the more. To the Jews I became as a Jew, in order to win Jews; to those under

[1] The sixth Article of Religion (*Book of Common Prayer*).

the law I became as one under the law—though not being myself under the law—that I might win those under the law. To those outside the law I became as one outside the law—not being without law toward God but under the law of Christ—that I might win those outside the law. To the weak I became weak, that I might win the weak. I have become all things to all men, that I might by all means save some.'[1]

You and I cannot bring men to God by whistling to them at a distance. We have to go and meet them, as God does, and psychologically speaking this means coming to them imaginatively where they imagine themselves to be. Do you remember how we read in Ezekiel 3. 15 that the prophet was sent upon a difficult mission to help men to discover where they really were in the eyes of God? In this passage I confess to thinking that the Authorized Version is a more faithful rendering than that of the Revised Standard Version. Following the Authorized Version we read,

'I came to them of the captivity . . . and I sat where they sat.'[2]

Moffatt renders it 'in the midst of them'. Another translation says 'conversant with them'. In each rendering, however, the suggestion is of meeting people where they think they are.

If, then, we are to evangelize men we must 'sit where they sit', 'be conversant with them', and the experience may be to us both an astonishment and an

---

[1] I Cor. 9. 19–22.
[2] R.S.V. renders this 'I sat there overwhelmed among them . . .'

overwhelming experience as it was to Ezekiel. It will certainly call for a most sensitive insight into the minds of those with whom we sit if we are to change their own understanding of their position to a true understanding.

To sit with men where they sit does not, of course, mean to think what they think. If we are true to the biblical understanding of man then we must see that what man thinks to be his greatest need is not necessarily his greatest need. Modern man is obsessed to-day with the need for security. We shall be far nearer to the biblical insight about man's condition if, with the American theologian Paul Tillich, we say that what man needs is not security but courage. And you will remember how, in his profoundly stimulating study, *The Courage to be*, Tillich brings his readers to the point of equating courage with faith.

Again we have only to recognize that we are no longer dealing with renaissance man, with man who thinks of himself as an individual, but with collectivized or 'conformist' man, to see how vastly complicated becomes the task of presenting the challenge of a God who calls each man by his name and looks for the response of trustful obedience by each man as a man.

How do we evangelize this new 'group' man? This is a question of urgent moment for the Church everywhere in the world, in America as in Europe, and not least in Asia and Africa. We do not, indeed, condemn man for being 'part' of society. We want him to be a 'part' of the divine society. But we have to be clear that to be part of the divine society involves courage. We must not facilely offer the Christian community as an alternative to man's other collectives. The Christian community is *not* a collective. It is a fellowship of the brave who live by faith.

We have only to ask these questions, and to see where even tentative answers are leading us, to recognize just how tremendous is the problem of communicating the gospel in our world to-day. At least it must be obvious that 'preaching' cannot be the only means of communication. As we study the other imperatives of the gospel we shall see how preaching is to be supplemented.

Meanwhile, however, an actual task confronts the preacher. He has to be not only heard but understood. For communication, as we have already stated, involves not only the transmission of the message, but also its reception in the sense of its being understood. Two illustrations may serve to indicate what is involved for the preacher.

In the first place he has to understand the images in which those to whom he preaches do their thinking. In the journal *Theology* there appeared early last year an article on the use by our Lord of parables. It began forcefully with a paragraph which reads—

'We can hardly deny that the incarnate Christ was the greatest theologian of them all. "He spake many things in parables" (Matt. 13. 3, 34, etc.). Our theology speaks in parables hardly at all, as a glance at the index of any theological journal will show. "The common people heard him gladly" (Mark 12. 37). They do not hear us gladly.'[1]

A large part of the article raises directly the issue of the translation of biblical language into the vernacular of our own day and time, and makes, in particular, a plea for a deliberate attempt by preachers to use parables which will convey a meaning to their hearers. He notes in the structure of parables two terms, the first fixed, the second variable. 'The latter', he says, 'is some person, thing, action or event, within the experience of his hearers. The fixed term, the Kingdom of Heaven, exactly fitted contemporary interests and aspirations . . . but in our contemporary industrial democracy the meaning of the phrase is virtually incommunicable to the uninitiated.'

This, of course, is not to insist that modern analogies to the Bible parables are either all the answer, or will in fact be anything but very difficult to come by. The article contains the shrewd reminder that—'As Jesus Himself served His thirty-year apprenticeship in contemporary village society, so maybe the parable-makers of to-morrow will have been born and bred on municipal housing estates.' What the writer is concerned to press home is that words which convey one reality to the preacher may convey quite another reality to the hearer. He gives a somewhat devastating illustration which nevertheless needs to be taken seriously. Speaking of the phrase 'the Kingdom of Heaven is like . . .' he says that to-day 'Kingdom,

[1] *The Power of Jesus is like . . .*, by A. H. Dammers, *Theology*, No. 404, February 1954, pp. 43–46.

Kingship, is divorced from sovereignty and power. Heaven is "my blue heaven"; or, more happily: "I'm in heaven, dancing cheek to cheek". Possibly a folk-memory survives of uncongenial harps and crowns.'

A subsequent article in the same journal takes up the challenge and tries to relate it to worship, the normal context of the preacher's activity. After suggesting a number of contemporary images and applying them to the wording of prayers, this other author continues by quoting from a hymn by Studdert Kennedy—'God in a workman's jacket as before'. That, he insists, says something to us that 'the Carpenter of Nazareth' cannot say. Then he asks:

'Is it perhaps the anachronism, the playing fast and loose with history that offends?' . . . He replies, 'We dare not say that if God had become incarnate at this time He could not or would not have become incarnate as a manual worker in heavy industry.'

He concludes with the query

'Is it not possible for the letter of historical propriety to obscure the spirit of theological relevance?'[1]

Elsewhere in the article he quotes with effect some words of Gregory Dix

'We must grasp the fact that worship cannot take place in an ecclesiastical Avalon, but to a large extent reflects the ever-changing needs and ideas of the worshippers.'[2]

If that is true of worship and the worshipper it is

[1] *More about Parables*, by Maurice Wiles, *Theology*, No. 411, September 1954, pp. 340–343.

[2] *The Shape of the Liturgy*, by Gregory Dix.

a fortiori true of the preacher and his hearers, if there is to be communication.

My second illustration is taken from the diary record of my visit to America last year. At one conference which I attended a speech was made which so impressed me that I managed to get most of it down. The speaker was describing how disconcerting it was to have to learn to rethink all one's categories. The record in the diary reads as follows—

'He described how a few years ago he was talking to an Asian group and quite failing to get anything across. After two days he said to them—"Now you tell me. What am I saying that seems to find no echo in your minds?" He then told us how those to whom he had been speaking had taken his vocabulary and showed him the associations for them of the words he used.'

'You talk', they said, 'about the danger of *dictatorship*. But we in Asia are not afraid of dictatorship. Most Asian people are illiterate. They want a leader. If they are not illiterate they still need leadership. To us what you fear is what we want.'

'You talk about *revolution* as if revolution was something bad. But for us revolution means change and for us change from the bad old ways is our desperate need.'

'You talk about crass *materialism*. Materialism for us means food and clothing and housing, and these are our basic needs. When you say materialism we say "goodie"!'

'You talk about *irreligion* and a way of life not based on faith. But in our experience the old religions supported the *status quo*. To be irreligious means for us to be against the *status quo*.'

I give that second illustration not only by way of an illuminating commentary on how important it is to

[36]

know what is the value given by the hearer to the words the preacher uses, but also to indicate that the mere use of non-biblical categories is no guarantee that one is speaking in such a way that the common people hear us gladly.

Perhaps I cannot do better in bringing this study of our first imperative to a close than quote some words from Dr. J. H. Oldham in his book *Life is Commitment* which is surely one of the most penetrating studies of the problem of communication published in this generation. He writes—

'If Christianity is to make headway to-day, Christians must learn to talk with those on the other side of the gulf. The Church seems to be hardly alive to the real situation. Christians go on talking freely about God, as though He might be taken for granted, whereas there are multitudes for whom the word "God" has lost all meaning whatsoever. It is useless to speak in a strange tongue. You cannot commend your faith to those who have no notion of what you mean. The first thing that needs to be done is to establish communication.'

He then continues with a sentence pregnant with meaning for us who would obey the imperative 'Go . . . preach'.

'If there is to be a genuine conversation between those on opposite sides of the gulf, Christians must be willing to listen as well as to teach.'[1]

We have here considered something of what is involved in obedience to the imperative 'Go preach'.

[1] *Life is Commitment*, by J. H. Oldham, 1953, p. 46.

We have seen that as ministers of reconciliation we
have to speak for God to man, and yet all the while
He is standing alongside men under the very Word we
speak. We speak and we listen. Except we listen we
cannot speak. We have to listen to God and to our
fellow-men. As men we speak to God in prayer. As
commissioned by God we speak 'in Christ' to men.
There is a picture of the preacher I would leave with
you in the words of a well-known poem of Charles
Sorley. In a sense rather different from his poem yet
not inconsistent with it we see the preacher—

> *With parted lips and outstretched hands*
> *And listening ears Thy servant stands,*
> *Call Thou early, call Thou late*
> *To Thy great service dedicate.*[1]

[1] *Expectans, Expectavi*, by Charles Sorley in *Marlborough and other Poems*, 1922, p. 68.

II

Go Teach

IN St. Matthew's recording of the great commission
we find our second imperative—'Go . . . and make
disciples of all nations . . . teaching them to observe all
that I have commanded you.'[1] That this command of
Jesus was obeyed by the Church long before St.
Matthew wrote his Gospel is made very clear from the
story of the missionary expansion of the Church in the
first generation after Pentecost. Something of the
intimacy with which this Christian imperative was
from the first linked to the one we have already considered, Go preach, may be gathered from the words
of Paul to the Romans—

> 'Thanks be to God, that you who were once slaves to sin
> have become obedient from the heart to the standard of
> teaching to which you were committed.'[2]

Behind that thanksgiving lies the undifferentiated
activity of the pioneer missionary who was preacher
and teacher, reconciler and priest in one, for whom
obedience to this imperative in all its many-sidedness
was the glory of the ministry which he describes in

[1] Matt. 28. 19–20.   [2] Rom. 6. 17.

such moving terms at the end of the first chapter of his letter to the Colossians. Having spoken of his 'divine office' as being 'to make the word of God fully known' he ends with this testimony—

> 'Him (the Christ) we proclaim, warning every man and teaching every man in all wisdom, that we may present every man mature in Christ.'[1]

Preaching merges into the task of education.

> 'For this I toil', says Paul, 'striving with all the energy which he mightily inspires within me.'[2]

How he toiled and how he strove at this work of education, how seriously the early Church took this imperative, has become much clearer to us thanks to the work of many recent New Testament scholars. They have established, surely beyond doubt, how much of the material in the Epistles, whether of Paul or others, represents a common source in the early catechetical material used for the instruction of enquirers. Nor need we doubt that the standard of teaching to which these enquirers were committed was itself profoundly shaped by the teaching of Jesus Himself, much of it later to be collected and arranged by Matthew in his Gospel. The imperative 'Go teach' was taken seriously from the first.

Our task is to see what this involves for the Mission of the Church to-day. Preliminary to this enquiry, however, we need to be clear that our obedience to the imperative 'Go teach' is directly linked to that of the Church whose obedience is on record in the New

[1] Col. 1. 28.   [2] Col. 1. 29.

Testament. There is a word used in the New Testament either as a verb *paradidōmi* or as a noun *paradosis* which is more commonly translated 'tradition' than 'teaching', a translation which has not been without its confusing effect in later debate. Tradition in its New Testament meaning signifies teaching which has been received and has been handed on. So Paul in writing to the Corinthians says—

'I received from the Lord what I also delivered (*paredōka*) to you, that the Lord Jesus on the night when he was betrayed took bread, and when he had given thanks he broke it. . . .'[1]

What Paul means is that the instruction about Holy Communion which he is giving is something he has himself been taught.

It is an associated usage, linked also with our imperative in St. Matthew's Gospel, which Paul has in his letter to the Philippians where he writes—

'What you have learned and received and heard and seen in me, do; and the God of peace will be with you.'[2]

One further quotation will suffice. It is taken from the passage in Paul's first letter to the Corinthians when he is about to give some of his most important teaching on death and resurrection. He prefaces this with a brief summary of the work of Christ, itself the nucleus of what may well have served as an early creed. He introduces this with the words, which we have already considered in another context—

'I would remind you, brethren, in what terms I preached to you the gospel, which you received, in which you

[1] I Cor. 11. 23.   [2] Phil. 4. 9.

[41]

stand, by which you are saved, if you hold it fast—
unless you believed in vain. For I delivered (*paredōka*)
to you as of first importance what I also received, that
Christ died for our sins in accordance with the scriptures, that he was buried, that he was raised on the
third day in accordance with the scriptures. . . .'[1]

Without labouring the point further I would draw
from these illustrations from the Epistles what I
believe is a legitimate conclusion with regard to the
apostolic teaching, as that is revealed in the early
missionary movement. The essence of that teaching is
not to be found in any code of ethics. Indeed, close
parallels to all the ethical teaching of the New Testament are to be found in Rabbinic Judaism, as in the
writings of classical antiquity, and in the sacred scriptures of the great religions of Asia. The essence of the
ethical teaching of the New Testament lies in its divine
perspective, in its direct relationship to the acts of God
in history which, culminating in the life, death and
resurrection of Jesus Christ, become the acts of God in
the life of the individual Christian and the Christian
community by the operation of the Holy Spirit.

Tradition, in the New Testament sense of the word,
can then be more properly equated with the word
Scripture itself, as we use the term, than with ecclesiastical custom treated as a supplement to Scripture.
So understood, the tradition which Paul and the other
early missionaries handed on, the content of their
teaching, was primarily a new perspective, in the light
of which religion and history, law and ethics, God and

[1] I Cor. 15. 1–4.

man, came to be viewed in a new light. For the first
missionary expansion of Christianity the really excit-
ing thing about any man is that if he is 'in Christ he is
a new creation; the old has passed away, behold, the
new has come.'[1]

This sense of a new perspective underlies the
Church's approach to the Bible and has done so from
the earliest days when that Bible, as yet, consisted
only of the Old Testament writings. In this the Church
derives its authority from the Christ Himself. The
Church was never to forget the experience of two of its
members on the late afternoon of the first Easter Day
when Jesus 'beginning with Moses and all the prophets
. . . interpreted to them in all the scriptures the things
concerning himself.'[2] It was in this tradition that we
see one of the first missionaries expounding Scripture.
'Do you understand what you are reading?' asked
Philip of the Ethiopian eunuch. 'How can I', he replied, 'unless someone guides me.' The word 'to guide'
(*hodēgeō*) is commonly used of 'to teach'. You will then
remember how, like a good teacher, Philip 'beginning
with the scripture', the fifty-third chapter of Isaiah
which the eunuch was studying, went on and 'told him
the good news of Jesus.'[3] The fact that in this incident
we see the missionary imperative in triple form, with
teaching and preaching and baptism all involved, does
not disguise the fact that the basic approach is that of
the teacher giving to the student a new perspective.

If we in our turn are to obey the command, 'Go
teach' we also must have what can, I think, properly

[1] II Cor. 5. 17.   [2] Luke 24. 27.   [3] Acts 8. 30-35.

be called this biblical perspective. By that I do not mean limiting our understanding to the degree of factual knowledge about the world, its natural order, its geography and its history enjoyed by those by whom the books of the Bible were first written or edited. And we are no more restricted to their psychology than we are to their cosmogony. The anatomy of the mind of man and of the universe in which he lives is still in our day something we can only see through a glass darkly. This was even more true for them. But we can share their perspective, the proportion in which they viewed the realities of human experience and the interpretation which they gave to them. It is possible to speak of their perspective in the singular because, for all the long span of history which they cover between them, they yet shared to a quite astonishing degree the same way of looking at things. They may indeed be considered, all of them, as painters of one 'school'. And that analogy may serve to show us our task in relation to them.

An American theologian, Dr. Paul Minear, introducing a study of the biblical perspective, makes this use of the analogy:

'In a painting perspectives may be dissociated—at least for the sake of analysis—from the objects depicted. One does not need to be an artist to distinguish some of the elements which combine to shape his perspective. It includes background and foreground, and their intricate and intimate interaction which conveys the actualities of depth and dimension. It involves the interplay of light and shadow, contrasts in colours which communicate the selectivity of vision. It incorporates a simple configuration of line and pattern, which one eye discerns among the many patterns which each setting affords. And these are unified by a single centre: the point at which the artist stands. Unless the onlooker stands at that centre he does not see the painting as the artist sees it. If there is to be communication, the onlooker need not share the painter's views but he must share the painter's *point of viewing*. He need not agree with his *standpoint*, but he must *stand* at the same *point*.'[1]

That analogy, like all analogies, cannot be pressed too far. But it serves to remind us that if we in our turn are to communicate to those we teach the perspectives of the Christian faith, of its interpretation of God and man and man's destiny, then we must take our stand at the point where those perspectives are most clearly enshrined, in that great picture gallery of faith which we call the Bible.

In elaborating this thought it is perhaps appropriate to quote from the Bishop of Bristol's Introduction to the London Syllabus of Religious Education, which serves as the agreed syllabus for use in the schools of the London County Council:

'Once we begin really to get the hang of the Bible,' he writes, 'we find in our hands certain great clues which, rightly followed, enable us to see the whole development in its true perspective and to distinguish essentials from non-essentials. Among these clues are such themes as the calling of the people of God, obedience and apostasy, the preservation of the true faith by a faithful remnant, the hope and the coming of Messiah, the great rejection, the calling of the new people of God, the Christian

[1] *Eyes of Faith—a Study in the Biblical Point of View*, by Paul S. Minear, 1946, p. 1.

[45]

Church. And through them all there runs the master-clue of history as God-centred. The whole drama is the drama of God's activity in Creation and Redemption.'[1]

All the lines are unified by a single centre, says Dr. Minear, 'the point at which the artist stands'. 'Through all', says the Bishop of Bristol, 'there runs the master-clue of history as God-centred.' They are saying the same thing and they are speaking about the same thing, the perspective of the Bible. As those who would obey the imperative 'Go teach' we take our stand at that centre.

From there we can see three lines running out to form the intricate pattern of our human life—the line of the individual, the line of the family, and the line of the community. In the biblical perspective each of these lines matters in the out-working of the divine purpose. These three, seen in biblical perspective, form the indispensable basis of Christian education.

In the midst of the turbulence of their world the biblical writers detected the activity of God directed towards themselves. 'The word of the Lord came . . .', that is not just third party description by an admiring posterity written long after the event. It is again and again the affirmation of the man for whom the coming of the Word was an utterly disconcerting and often a most disagreeable experience, a prelude to innumerable dangers and often death. In this activity of God dealing with persons as persons, as those capable of a responsible obedience, these writers discovered the real

[1] *The London Syllabus of Religious Education*, with Introduction by the Bishop of Bristol, 1947, p. 19.

significance of man. All genuine moral growth springs from that insight. We to-day live in a world, by far the most serious danger in which is the widespread assault on the value of human personality. This assault may be the assault of totalitarian tyranny using psychological techniques which break a man's integrity from within. It is no less an assault when it takes the subtler form of conforming men to a common social pattern through the techniques of mass production, and so more slowly, though not necessarily less thoroughly, dispossesses them of their birthright of individuality. In such a world there is no finer source of inspiration for our share in the resistance to, and victory over this peril than to draw deeply upon the perspective of the biblical writers, who, more clearly than any others in human history, first asserted the moral significance of the individual, gave him his true dignity as a child of God.

Yet for all its emphasis on the importance of the individual as a responsible person, the biblical perspective is never content to leave the individual in isolation. It is true to this biblical insight that in the two stories of creation as recorded in the book Genesis we see man and woman, either viewed as part of one creative act, or as essentially complementary to one another, precisely because 'it is not good that the man should be alone'.[1] There is more than poetry in the Psalm which speaks of God 'setting the solitary in families' or as Moffatt puts it 'God who brings the lonely home'.[2] What we have here is the deep con-

[1] Gen. 2. 18. [2] Ps. 68. 6. A.V.

viction that man, if he is to be fully man must be man-in-fellowship.

Here is the true inwardness of the historic chain which sees Abraham, the Patriarchs, and Israel as the archetype of the individual, the family, and the community. These are the primary elements of human history in every time and place. The biblical perspective takes these three elements seriously and makes their interaction and the action of God upon them the key to the understanding of man and God's purpose for him. This purposeful history is interpreted by the Bible as a drama which takes up into itself individual, family and community, seeing all of these redeemed in Christ and liberated by Him to fulfil God's purpose of salvation.

This perspective, in turn, yields another point of view of great importance. The golden age of the Bible is not in the past. It is in the future. The Bible is shot through and through with a great hopefulness. Precisely because it takes history seriously, it takes man as he is, takes all the evil in man's life and his environment and discovers there God working out His purpose of goodness. In and through man as he is, in and through the evil that is in the world the Bible sees God at work bringing to pass a complete at-one-ment between Himself and man, and between man and man.

That is the strange history at the centre of which the writers of the Bible stood. Part of the teaching mission of the Church consists in seeking to bring men and women to an awareness that that is the true history in which they too stand.

[48]

With that perspective, against the background of that understanding of history, we can proceed to some consideration of what is involved in the imperative 'go teach' as that is applied in the Christian Mission to pre-Christian society in Asia and Africa to-day. In thus limiting our theme I do so both because it will make it more compassable and because such knowledge as I may possess is largely confined to this field. But even in limiting what I have to say to Asia and Africa I am very much aware of the extent to which the educational problem in these continents is itself complicated by the confusion of the West and by the lack of any clear Christian philosophy of education either in Europe or America. For whether it be in the Sciences or the Humanities, the East and Africa are still going to school in Europe and America. That fact carries with it this assurance, that in obeying the imperative 'go teach' we will be only a little less involved with Asia and Africa if we remain in Massachusetts or the Middle West, London or Liverpool, than if we went to the Philippines or Liberia, to Singapore or the Gold Coast.

As a clue through the labyrinth of education as that is both understood and misunderstood in Asia and Africa, the Christian teacher has to his hand the three lines we have already considered—the individual, the family and the community. In fidelity to the biblical perspective with regard to these three, he, or she, has a standard of measurement by which all achievement as well as the goal must be judged.

Among the peoples of Asia and Africa, thanks in

large measure to pressure from the West, economic, cultural and political, there has been, over recent years, a transition from a condition of society based on 'status' to a society based on 'contract'. In a society of the first kind a man's place in life is assured at birth and is unlikely to change. In a society of the second kind a man's place in life is determined by his success or failure in competition with his fellows. The individual finds his own level, it is not found for him. Broadly speaking, the caste system of India and the tribal system of Africa can be taken as examples of social life based on 'status'. The characteristic position of the individual in post-feudal western society is an example of a society based on 'contract', or if you will, competition.

From the point of view of the teacher the task of education in a society in transition is as profoundly complicated as it is spiritually challenging. Whether he is dealing with children or with adults he is dealing with persons who are adrift from their moorings. For such the description of their society as a disintegrating one is no facile cliché but a poignant reality. Manifestly the task of guiding such individuals is vastly more difficult than is the case with those whose society has long since successfully made the transition. It is further complicated by the fact that the peoples of Asia and Africa have been, or still are, in a colonial or semi-colonial status over against those western societies whose impact upon them has set in process this avalanche of change. To all the other strains of transition is added the struggle for independence. This, in turn, is aggravated by another factor. Peoples in a stage of transition are, in terms of power, at a disadvantage in relation to peoples who have already accomplished the necessary adjustment. This disadvantage adds an emotional factor of extreme bitterness.

In his enquiry into the aims of education, published a few years ago under the title *Glaucon*, Professor M. V. C. Jeffreys, Professor of Education in Birmingham, has some important things to say. Albeit speaking of the situation in western society, what he says is relevant to Asia and Africa. He discovers in a disintegrating society three areas of need in which the Christian teacher has to act.

First there is, he says, a need for 'a double redemption, of the individual and of society—of the bewildered individual from depersonalization and of the planned society from tyranny.'[1] The importance of that observation for the pre-Christian society, which we are considering, is in the reminder that it offers that to be a man of two worlds and at home in neither is one form of depersonalization. For such a man does not belong anywhere. He is 'isolated, alone, and afraid'. He can deny social responsibility and plunge into the anarchy of individualism. Or he can sacrifice liberty to security. The modern history of China in the last forty years is only the experience of the average Chinese peasant writ large on a national scale. Having tasted the anarchy of individualism he was prepared to sacrifice liberty to security. That is the context in

[1] *Glaucon*, by M. V. C. Jeffreys, 1950, p. 55.

which the Christian who, in China to-day, seeks to obey the imperative 'go teach' has to be obedient. The costliness of such a task for such a Christian should serve as a sobering challenge to us, who are not so confined, to see our mission as teachers in this doubly redemptive role.

The *second* area of need to which Professor Jeffreys draws our attention is that which calls for 'not only a literate but an educated people'. 'If it is true', he continues, 'that universal education had to be undertaken because society had reached a stage of development at which it could no longer work unless people could read and write, it is no less true that we have now reached a stage of development at which our society will not work unless people can do a great deal more.'[1]

The problem posed by Professor Jeffreys is vastly aggravated in Asia and Africa because not only are their societies in the transition we have already noted, but educationally speaking there is a vast demand for every stage of education, from literacy to University level, by peoples who see in education the goal of all their hopes, the answer to all their fears. Not only are millions learning to read and write, but great numbers are pressing forward for Professor Jeffreys' 'something more'.

A recent very thorough review of the development of educational facilities in British Tropical Africa sounded two warnings, amongst many others, though without much hope that they would be heeded by the education-hungry peoples to whom they were ad-

[1] M. V. C. Jeffreys, op. cit., p. 68.

dressed. The warnings, however, bear so directly on the contribution of the Christian teachers that they should receive our careful attention.

The Report says:

'One of the biggest dangers threatening the healthy growth of education on the West Coast is that the demand for secondary education will be met by the opening of new so-called secondary schools which have neither the staff nor the buildings which are essential if the pupils are to receive a proper secondary education. In both these matters the laying down and enforcing of sound minimum standards is essential. To lay down standards which are not always enforced and which, even if they were, are so low as to give a cloak of rectitude to schools the very existence of which is, in fact, a scandal, may produce a temporary slackening of political pressure but must produce ultimate educational disaster.'[1]

The second warning is expressed laconically in one brief sentence:

'On the trustworthiness of the local administration the whole future of West African education depends.'[2]

Those warnings are recorded in order to present as dramatically as possible the painful dilemma confronting the Christian teacher in places where educational facilities are far from corresponding with the demand. The tensions for such a teacher are often quite unbearable, especially if he comes from the West himself. There is the immediate tension between the principles

[1] *African Education—a Study of Educational Policy and Practice in British Tropical Africa*, 1953, p. 26.
[2] Op. cit. p. 12.

[53]

of quantity and quality presented by a time-table which normally calls for a staff that does not exist. There is the further tension between the duty owed to every pupil, and the possibilities of the few for a leadership which the local and national community desperately needs. Beyond these is the tension involved in being an alien who is needed but not wanted, and whose educational idealism as well as Christian standards are more likely to be the objects of suspicion than of admiration. All of these tensions, we may observe, have to be experienced in a society in transition, without landmarks, without the fundamental psychic securities which provide for peace of mind and which, in a stable community, are taken for granted.

Paradoxically Professor Jeffreys' *third* area of need offers to the Christian teacher not just another demand but a way of hope.

> 'Once a man claims individual responsibility, or has it thrust upon him', says Professor Jeffreys, 'his social relations must be at a rational and moral, that is a fully personal, level. . . . By affirming his individuality man necessarily makes the problem of community a more difficult one by raising it to a higher plane.'

When I say that this affords a way of hope I am not under-estimating the great undertaking involved for the Christian teacher who, by the very process of educating people for the world to-day, has to substitute conscious responsibility of choice for the sub-personal responses dictated by tribal or caste rules. The way of hope lies precisely at the point where the new demand seems most inexorable, in its insistence that community has to be realized on a higher plane.

In a word we have got to see the essential nature of the imperative 'go teach' as being always vastly greater than anything which can be encompassed in a classroom or a school. The lines of the individual and the family and the community have got to intersect if we are going to achieve through education a successful transition from an old dissolving society to a new stable one.

This at once poses tremendous questions for the Christian Church as a whole, as well as for those Christians whose particular vocation it has been to embody their obedience to the command 'go teach' in the field of formal education. Having the pre-Christian society of Asia and Africa still in the forefront of our minds, we have to remember that in both these continents western education was, with few exceptions, pioneered by Christian missionaries. In Africa it would be safe to say that there were no exceptions. Indeed even to-day the greater part of primary education in Tropical Africa, and a substantial percentage of secondary education, is still under the auspices of the Church. That those receiving any education at all still represent only a small proportion of the number of children of school age does not affect the significance of what the Church has attempted.

This record of past achievement represents to-day a real embarrassment to the Church in the way of its freedom to meet what we see is embodied in the true understanding of the imperative to teach—the drawing of persons out of isolation into a community of the highest, richest and most satisfying kind. In Asia the Church is embarrassed because its character as a very small minority has only recently been exposed. Previous to the achievement of effective political independence, all the colonial or semi-colonial territories of Asia were under the control of western powers. China was no exception, for there economic and cultural control were as effective as political domination elsewhere. These circumstances, while securing for the Christian communities both prestige and protection, obscured their real position. In the successor states, all of them in varying degrees animated by a nationalism whose symbol is a revival of traditional religion, or as in China the establishment of the new 'religion' of Communism, the Christian minority is nervous as to its future. Education, in such a situation, however thinly veneered with Christianity, is felt to be infinitely better than education under exclusively Hindu, Muslim, Buddhist, or secular auspices. And who is to challenge that conclusion? Yet, in practice, the understanding in the Asian churches of what education means tends to be limited to what happens at school and in the class-room. Resources are not readily released to be made available for the wider task of the Church in creating a community of such a quality that its witness will have a commanding influence on the non-Christian world around it. That remains an embarrassing fact when viewed in the light of the imperative to 'go teach', as we have already seen it expressed in the New Testament, and as the most experienced Christian educationists of to-day are clearly understanding it.

In Africa the embarrassment of the Church is to be traced to another cause. Here, in the first place, prestige is involved. The mere fact that what western education has been available in Tropical Africa has been provided by Christian schools means that educated Africans, and notably the leaders in the nationalist movements in Africa, are still, in the great majority of cases, Christians at least by profession. While gratitude is not, and never has been, a political virtue, and in Africa, as elsewhere, it would be folly to presume on it, yet the contribution of the Church in the field of school education is widely appreciated. At a moment when more and more school education, regardless of the best educational advice and in defiance of the best educational standards, is everywhere demanded, the Church is confronted with a most painful dilemma. If it yields to the pressure it will share in the educational disaster involved. It will be quite unable to build a community giving the witness of 'a city set on a hill', the kind of qualitative witness that is needed by disintegrating communities involved in the difficult transition from tribal societies to modern nation-states. On the other hand if it refuses to yield it will certainly become very unpopular, as being unpatriotic, and liable to suspicion, as being under foreign influences anti-pathetic to national independence. But not only that, it may well see a large part of its traditional structure disorganized by the withdrawal of grants from its schools, or the wholesale taking over of the schools by the State. Only those who understand the place of the village school-*cum*-church and the significance of the teacher-*cum*-evangelist in the structure of both Christian education and the life of the Church in Africa, can fully appreciate the magnitude of the issues involved. The embarrassment to the Church, however, remains. Nothing like enough attention is being paid by the Church in Africa to the achievement of a high level of community life. Resources for this are not made available or, where available, are grudged if it is thought that they might be used to establish one more school.

The command 'go teach' remains a Christian imperative. If we are right in our main emphasis as to what is involved in obedience: if, with Professor Jeffreys, we recognize the need for a double redemption of the individual and society: if we see that education comprises more than book learning: if we see the vision of a community like a city set on a hill which cannot be hid: then we must infuse into all our thinking about the task of the teacher a new perspective. And this new perspective will have, in turn, to be diffused far and wide through the life of the Church, not only in Asia and Africa, but also in the West, to which, in one way or another, Asia and Africa still come to school. Teaching we have to see as part of the commission of Christ to His Church. We shall best see it in perspective if we see it as an activity discharged by the Christian community, working, indeed, through individuals specially denominated as teachers, but not only through them. The family is a school and so is the wider life of society within which the family is set. Above all the Church at worship is a school. No one of these can be isolated from the rest without loss. Each can only achieve its full usefulness as an organ of obedience to the divine imperative if it is seen in association with the others. Thus individual and family and Church are merged in a community of obedience.

Something of the magnitude of what is involved in the imperative 'go teach' has here been indicated. Something of the confusion which obscures the nature of the task has been briefly outlined. Something of the way of fulfilment has been described. But I think that if you have followed me so far you will have a ready and kindly sympathy for an old African whose remark was reported to me some years ago when I was travelling in the Kikuyu country of Kenya. The old man had been pondering for some while in silence on the subject of education and the problems it was raising for his people. Finally he broke his silence with the words, 'The pursuit of education is rather like hunting ivory; when you get it you find there is an elephant attached to it!'

At the risk of being trampled on, however, we must go on hunting for ivory. Only so will the messianic vision of the psalmist be fulfilled and the 'ivory palaces'[1] of an Asia, an Africa, and a world redeemed echo with the praises of God.

[1] Ps. 45. 8.

[59]

III

Go Heal

A CAREFUL study of what the Bible has to say about healing suggests that the imperative 'go heal' may well open up vistas of service which almost make it a synonym for the Church's total obedience to the divine commission. In his great vision of that which *is*, as well as that which *is to come*, the writer of the Apocalypse shows us

> 'the river of the water of life, bright as crystal, flowing from the throne of God and of the Lamb through the middle of the street of the City; also on either side of the river, the tree of life with its twelve kinds of fruit, yielding its fruit each month; and the leaves of the tree are for the healing of the nations.'[1]

F. D. Maurice is surely right in refusing to treat this vision as being but a glimpse into the future. The New Testament writers for all their expectancy, for all the hope by which they were encouraged, were yet men whose primary concern was their present discipleship. Indeed their very hope rested upon the realities of the past and the actualities of the present. Their eager anticipation of things to come was an *a fortiori* argu-

[1] Rev. 22. 1–2.

ment from the good already experienced, not a compensation. 'This *is* eternal life'[1] they could say, because they had already come to know the only God and Jesus Christ whom He had sent. 'We know that we have passed out of death into life, because we love the brethren'[2]—that was their claim. 'In Christ . . . the old has passed away . . . the new has come'[3]—that was their certainty. Paul's whole argument in Galatians, chapter 4 is concerned with the present citizenship of the New Jerusalem. 'The Jerusalem above is free, and she is our mother . . . brethren, we are not children of the slave but of the free woman. For freedom Christ has set us free.'[4]

Maurice has all that and much more behind him to justify his comment on Revelation 22. 1–2:

'The river of life is that which quickens, invigorates, unites a society of men, made to partake of God's likeness. The tree of life is He whom they behold, He in whom they see the perfection of their own estate, He from whom all vital power descends upon them . . . the Son of God is the Source of those different graces which all have received, grace for grace; who distributes His twelve manner of fruits in the proportions and at the times which are suitable to the characters and circumstances of each society or each man; who overshadows with His leaves those to whom the taste of the fruits is unknown; who makes all the outward ministrations of His Gospel and Church serviceable for the cure of the miseries which selfishness has inflicted upon the nations.'[5]

[1] John 17. 3. [2] I John 3. 14. [3] II Cor. 5. 17.
[4] Gal. 4. 26, 31; 5. 1.
[5] *Lecture on the Apocalypse*, F. D. Maurice, 1861, pp. 429-430.

Through that vision we gain a true perspective of the healing ministry of the Church in its magnificent range. Here is a service without limit. Indeed it is perhaps not without some significance, as indeed it may well be not without encouragement to us all, to note that the two words *therapeia* and *latreuō*, which appear in the record of this vision, the one referring to the healing of the nations, and the other in a later verse to the worship given by the citizens to God, both have as their basic meaning, 'service'. We remember that 'servant' is one of the greatest of all the words of biblical religion. The healing ministry, indeed, in its essence is the healing ministry of Christ Himself mediated through His Church to the world as the Church obeys the command 'go heal'.

If then we understand the imperative 'go heal' as involving an obedience without limit, how are we to understand what is meant by healing? What follows is not an attempt to search the Bible for its use of medical terms. Rather I would invite you to distinguish certain emphases which together make up what the Bible signifies by 'healing'. There would seem to be three of these. The distinction between them is to be understood, however, on the basis of analysis and not of verbal form. Interesting as the nuances of meaning between the Greek words used may be, and suggestive as these often are, too much cannot be built upon them. In the case of our analysis there is a considerable overlap in the terms used.

The *first* emphasis is that which sees the whole personality in the full range of its need. Man's basic illness lies in his being divided from God, separated from his neighbour, at cross purposes with himself. Spiritual, mental and physical instability is the result. Salvation according to the Bible is the restoration of man to his true harmony with God, with his neighbour and himself. This is at-one-ment as the Bible understands it. This fundamental conception governs all such references as 'The Son of Man came to seek and to save the lost'[1]; 'I am the door; if anyone enters by me, he will be saved',[2] a saying shortly followed by the definition of 'being saved'—'I came that they may have life and have it abundantly'[3]; with, of course, the 'great inclusive' of John 3. 16–17 where salvation and eternal life are equated. The verb 'to save' in all these passages is *sōzō*. And this verb is also used in a number of instances in which Jesus healed the sick. It is, at the very least, highly suggestive that in every[4] case where this verb is used of a healing work of Jesus it is in an instance where stress is laid on the response of the sick person, whatever the nature of the malady. Faith is the great integrative principle in man which responds to the divine integrating power of grace.

Here then is an emphasis on the healing of sickness, whether of body or mind or spirit, or of all three at the same time, as being something closely associated with what the New Testament means by salvation.

[1] Luke 19. 10.   [2] John 10. 9.   [3] John 10. 10.

[4] Matt. 9. 21 may perhaps be held to justify the claim that Mark 6. 56 is no exception to the rule that where *sōzō* is used, there was in the one healed a response of faith.

Before leaving the consideration of this first emphasis of the biblical idea of healing it is important to remember that in the New Testament salvation is not just the rescue of man from a predicament, a great escape from a great peril, but is essentially the entering by man into a right relationship with God and so with his neighbour and himself. And the rightness of the relationship consists in this, that God reckons that the response of faith, trust in His grace, is the righteousness for which He looks and upon which all other relationships depend. Only on the basis of such an equation can the injunction 'you shall be holy for I am holy'[1] transcend a merely formal and ritual significance and be a determinant for life. Holiness, so understood, is a correlative of wholeness, of being healed, in a profoundly theological sense.[2]

The *second* emphasis is one which deals with the community as a social and political entity. We have already seen that the community, as well as the individual, is the object of the divine compassion and the healing mercy of God, from the vision of the nation's being healed in Revelation, chapter 22. We shall be considering in a moment the other very significant New Testament view of healing in relation to the community. But in this particular emphasis the most striking evidence is from the Old Testament, where in a sense in which it is not true of the New

[1] Lev. 11. 44–45; I Peter 1. 16.

[2] The fact that in Old English the words 'holy', 'whole' and 'heal' are found to share the same root is linguistically interesting. But it is only a biblical theology which establishes a living contemporary relationship between the words.

Israel, the Old Israel was, as a nation, a social and political entity.

In the record of Solomon's prayer after the building of the temple we are told of God's answer in which the phrase occurs:

'If my people who are called by my name humble themselves, and pray and seek my face, and turn from their wicked ways, then I will hear from heaven, and will forgive their sin and heal their land.'[1]

In this striking passage the common life of the nation is seen as intimately related to the very soil on which they live. The soul of a people and the soil of a people are never very far separated from one another in the biblical perspective. Man's relationship with nature is decisively affected for good or evil by his relationship with God. There is more than a play on words when we say that soul-erosion and soil-erosion are two related symptoms of human maladjustment. Healing then is related to the whole nexus of the people's life. That would have seemed as obvious to an ancient Hebrew as it is still obvious to the peasant masses of mankind. Forgiveness, at-one-ment, embraces the whole of life. It is the readjustment of the maladjusted.

Two other illustrations may be taken in which the forgiveness of God restores not only individuals but an apostate community. In Isaiah we read of

'the day when the Lord binds the hurt of his people, and heals the wounds inflicted by his blow.'[2]

Perhaps more striking still is the assurance given to

[1] II Chron. 7. 14. [2] Isa. 30. 26.

Jeremiah, while still imprisoned in the beleaguered city, that God is going to bring His own triumphant purpose out of the apparent utter frustration of His will by His disobedient people. Immediate disaster lies ahead but that is not the end:

> 'Behold, I will bring to it health and healing', saith the Lord, 'and I will heal them and reveal to them abundance of prosperity and security.'[1]

In these passages, typical as they are of many others throughout the Old Testament, we have the biblical insistence that a group, a nation, the State, possesses a real personality. Readers of Dr. Vidler's book *The Orb and the Cross* will remember the chapter entitled 'Is the State a "Moral Personality"?' and the conclusion to which he comes that some such term must be accepted if we are to consider the State as having the capacity for moral responsibility.

> 'The essence of the unity of a group', he says, 'is most adequately described as a person rather than as a purpose. The State is not merely a thing or object for us to use; through it a group-personality addresses us.'[2]

Following his argument Dr. Vidler would certainly consider that the group-personality, being morally accountable, is at all times addressed by God. We may as certainly say that this is the assumption of the Bible. This second emphasis on the moral responsibility of any human grouping and therefore its need for forgiveness and healing has, as we shall see later,

[1] Jer. 33. 6.
[2] *The Orb and the Cross*, A. R. Vidler, 1945, p. 66, note 4.

far-reaching significance for the Christian obedience to the imperative 'go heal'.

The *third* emphasis in what the Bible signifies by healing relates to the life of the New Israel. In two passages which, in their turn, have important implications, we see how, within the life of the Church, the individual and corporate aspects of healing, already considered, are intended to find their demonstration.

In writing to the Galatians, Paul has just concluded his triumphant argument about the Christian life as life in the Spirit. But with his characteristic ability to have his head in the clouds and his feet on solid earth, he can move straight from the assumption that the Christian does live by the Spirit to the observed fact that he also grieves the Spirit by the way in which so easily he breaks fellowship with other Christians. Then comes a passage of great tenderness which takes us as surely into the heart of the Beloved Community as any other. He writes:

> 'Brethren, if a man is overtaken in any trespass, you who are spiritual should restore him in a spirit of gentleness.'[1]

The rendering 'overtaken in a trespass' or, as the Authorized Version has it, 'overtaken in a fault', quite unnecessarily softens the significance of what Paul is saying. As translated it might indeed denote, for us to-day, no deeper content than being stopped by a speed-cop after being overtaken in the fault of travelling too fast in some restricted area. What Paul

[1] Gal. 6. 1.

is saying is that if a brother is found sinning, then he is to be restored in a spirit of gentleness, such as we could not be sure of finding in a speed-cop.

What Paul is concerned with is the disrupting power of sin, which not only breaks the fellowship between God and man, but also that between man and his fellows. The prescription for the treatment is gentleness born of humility. The breach is to be healed. The wound in the life of the fellowship is to be bound up. All that we have seen of the relationship of forgiveness with healing is here involved. Without making too much of the point it is interesting to note that the verb 'to restore' is *katartidzō*, which is also the technical medical term for the setting of a broken limb. The association of the word 'gentleness' with the word 'restore' would suggest that the medical use of the term may not have been foreign to Paul's thought in the moment of writing.

The other passage comes in Paul's first letter to the Corinthians. He has been deeply distressed to hear that the very unity of the Church is in danger of being disrupted by schism. The body of Christ is being divided, as men quarrel over the respective merits of different teachers and spiritual leaders. The long and tragic story of Christian disunity is here seen in its beginnings. To these divided Christians Paul writes:

'I appeal to you, brethren, by the name of our Lord Jesus, that all of you . . . . . be united in the same mind and the same judgment.'[1]

[1] I Cor. 1. 10.

What Paul is calling for is the restoration of harmony, the at-one-ment amongst brethren for whom at-one-ment with God has been established as he has just reminded them. 'God is faithful', he has just said, 'by whom you were called into the fellowship of his Son, Jesus Christ our Lord'.[1] The breach must be healed. The surgical analogy is perhaps not present here as in the Galatians passage but it is interesting that the same verb *katartidzō* is used for 'be united'.

That disunity was thought of in terms of sickness in the early Church can certainly be inferred from that other passage when, in the same letter to the same Corinthians, Paul is dealing with the crowning infamy of their disunity, that they even allow their divisions to separate between them at the Holy Communion. The context of those solemn words—

'Whoever, therefore, eats the bread or drinks the cup of the Lord in an unworthy manner will be guilty of profaning the body and blood of the Lord'—

is a division in the Church, partly social but partly, it would seem, related to the quarrels about which he wrote at the beginning of the letter. What is noteworthy is that, immediately following the searching words about 'unworthy eating', there comes the conclusion 'That is why many of you are weak and ill, and some have died'.[2]

The implication is that a worthy partaking of the sacrament of unity is itself unifying, life-giving, conducive to healing, is efficacious towards making both

[1] I Cor. 1. 9. [2] I Cor. 11. 30.

individual and community whole—is a veritable 'medicine of immortality'. Seeing that the Church is intended by the Lord to demonstrate its unity so that the world may believe, seeing that the Sacrament of the Body and Blood of Christ drew into a mysterious unity with one another and their Lord the quarrelling disciples, in the midst of whose disputing it was first instituted, it remains at least arguable that the weight of the New Testament evidence justifies our taking some risks with the Sacrament and allowing it to help in the healing of our divisions today.

Our study of the biblical significance of healing must now yield to a consideration of how this understanding is to be applied in our day as we seek to obey the imperative 'go heal'. Before we make the transition, however, and for our sobering it is necessary for us to remember that the way of healing, as the Bible understands it, is infinitely costly. The Bible offers no facile diagnosis of the sickness of mankind. 'The heart is deceitful above all things, and desperately corrupt',[1] says Jeremiah. The Septuagint version, you remember, softens this considerably but adds the subtle touch, 'The heart is the man'. The Old Testament is the tragic record of how a community could so persistently ignore the visitations of God, whether recognized as mercy or as judgment, that there came a day when the blindness of Israel became complete and the Messiah was crucified between two thieves. Individually and collectively we must accept the verdict of the Psalmist

[1] Jer. 17. 9.

who speaks for God who, looking at mankind, finds that 'they have all gone astray, they are all alike corrupt'.[1] So it is that Isaiah looks into the mystery of redemption and sees One who—

> 'has borne our griefs and carried our sorrows; . . . wounded for our transgressions, he was bruised for our iniquities; upon him was the chastisement that made us whole, and with his stripes we are healed.'[2]

To share in the healing ministry of Christ involves 'the fellowship of his sufferings'.[3] Paul could even have it as an ambition to become 'like him in his death',[4] meaning thereby a complete self-offering of obedience. It is with that in our minds, as the standard of our ministry, that we must seek to grasp what it means for the Church and for the Christian to 'go heal' in the world to-day.

From the foregoing analysis of the biblical emphases on healing, the task of the Church can be seen as threefold. Individuals have to be healed. From being isolated in sin, insulated by fear, they have to be restored to fellowship with God and with their fellows. Communities of men also need healing, need to be adjusted internally by the establishment of a righteous order and externally, in relation to other communities, by the recognition of the transcending authority of God. In both these enterprises the Church is involved by virtue of its Mission: but neither can be fulfilled except the Church, in its own life, be able to demon-

[1] Ps. 14. 3.   [2] Isa. 53, 4, 5   [3] Phil. 3. 10. A.V.
[4] Phil. 3. 11.

strate that it is indeed the society of the divine forgiveness within which men and women who have been
forgiven learn how to forgive and so create a genuine
community in which mutual dependence, mutual consideration and mutual helpfulness are a living standard of obedience.

In every generation the Church has discovered how
difficult is the task of obedience and how costly. What
no generation is entitled to say is that its task is more
difficult than that of previous generations. In truth its
task may well be very different in some particulars
from that of any generation which has gone before.
But likewise it will possess assets different from and,
in some respects, greater than theirs. We have, for
instance, had a longer experience of the grace of God
than the Church which saw the disintegration of the
Roman Empire. We forget that the Dark Ages looked
far more impossible from the point of view of those
who were entering them than they do from where we
stand with our knowledge of how a great Christian
culture emerged from that darkness. If we, too, are
entering another period of dissolution and if the constructive period still lies far ahead, we have in the
records of the divine mercy 'a cordial for drooping
spirits'—of even stronger proof than any previous
generation possessed.

In some respects perhaps our greatest difficulty
today lies within ourselves, in our defective sense
of historical proportions, in our inability, even yet,
to dissociate our minds from the complacencies

generated by a century of astonishingly rapid
material progress to which our whole outlook has
been accommodated. Here, surely, within ourselves,
must be our main difficulty, for otherwise how are
we to explain the persistence of political and economic
and religious illusions on the part of leaders and led
alike over so much of our western world? Prepared
then to acknowledge that we are slow to read the signs
of the times, let us consider the immediate impact of
some of the movements of our time upon our Mission.

A vast tearing up of human communities by their
roots has been in progress for more than a century and
a half and is proceeding at hurricane force. Beginning
in the West with the migration of peasantry into new
industrial agglomerations and then overseas, the uprooting has been continued by two world wars and the
mass migrations which have been their sequel. But
this is only to speak of the uprooting of men's bodies
from the familiar environment in which they and their
fathers had lived for generations. Given time the
migrant has put down roots again as Americans have
demonstrated both more successfully and on a larger
scale than any other people. But the greater part of
the uprooted have not had the good fortune to become
American citizens.

Meanwhile, on a far vaster scale there has been an
uprooting of the mind and spirit. The revolution that
is now in progress, in the mind of Asia, is far more than
a protest against subordination to the West. The real
revolution in Asia is the bringing to the end of millennia
of inertia based on religious concepts which made

development impossible. When the Muslim masses cease to believe in Kismet, and the Hindu masses cease to believe in Karma, and the Buddhist masses cease to believe that all desire is vanity, and the disciples of Confucius and Lao Tze turn to follow Karl Marx and Lenin and Mao-tse-tung, something is happening besides which the much advertised revolt against colonialism is seen to be little more than a desperate attempt to gain breathing space for the tremendous challenge of construction that the future holds.

What is happening in Africa we do not know. A notable leading article in the London *Times* for January 1, 1955, under the title 'In a glass darkly' made this comment on Africa:

> 'Africa, with all the progress that has taken place, remains essentially a continent of mystery. Amidst all the welter of words that comes from the Union and from the Colonial territories the Africans are a people who have not spoken yet. No-one knows what they are really thinking. No-one can forecast the outcome of the two widely different experiments in racial relations being made in the central and southern parts of the continent. At present the world has more urgent pre-occupations; but none more important. Africa simmers. This will not always be so. We are conscious mostly of the evil of Mau Mau; we should not ignore its significance.'

Part at least of the significance of Mau Mau, as of all that is happening in Africa, is, perhaps, to be understood as a profound racial frustration based on a progressive disillusionment which is nourished by fear. A distinguished English psychologist of considerable experience in East Africa, Dr. Carothers, has recently been engaged in an attempt to analyse the psychic factors that lie behind the Mau Mau outburst in Kenya. In his conclusion he lays stress on the fact that Africa today is in a stage of transition. Defining this term he has occasion, you will be interested to notice, to quote from an American writer, Faris, on the behaviour disorders of American cities. Faris, as quoted by Dr. Carothers, says:

'Such research of a scientific character as has dealt with the relation between ecology and behaviour has mainly been concerned with social disorganization and the consequent form of personal disorganization. This disorganization is for the most part a phenomenon of a great transition . . . such movements break up the social systems that control and integrate the behaviour of persons, so that new, unconventional and abnormal types of behaviour appear. These abnormalities are not essentially aspects of city life, or civilized society, but rather of the populations which are changing from one system to another.'

Dr. Carothers continues:

'The shock in Africa is much more drastic. African societies have presumably never been quite static; no utterly static organization could survive for long. But it is of the essence of all pre-literate cultures that their survival (as pre-literate cultures) depended on gradualness of change. Such gradual changes have occurred in Africa by the influence of contiguous tribes upon each other, as with the Masai and the Kikuyu. But it has become only too clear that when European influence impinges on the African, his whole cultural machinery is apt to collapse quite quickly.'[1]

[1] *The Psychology of Mau Mau*, J. C. Carothers, 1954, p. 6.

Cautioning us to treat the application of that generalization with a due regard for exceptions, Dr. Carothers disputes the prevalent assumption that western education, in the formal sense, has been a major factor in the breakdown of African life. Rather he sees the life of the African as 'mainly governed by the question of power'. The powerlessness of the African's traditional resources to combat the impact of the European's new ideas has led the African to an attempt to acquire the European's secret of power. This, Dr. Carothers would see as lying at the back of the passionate pursuit of European education by Africans and the mounting frustration as awareness dawns that book learning of the kind, and to the extent available, possesses no magic properties yielding power.

The frustration at a lack of power and disillusionment at the failure to acquire power, these stimulated by anxieties about land, for the African the ultimate basis of his psychic security, and fear of famine as a by no means remote possibility—all these lie behind the abnormality of Mau Mau. They explain how flagrant violations of some of the most rigid 'tabus' of the Kikuyu, 'abnormalities', can coincide with what also takes the form of a revival of paganism, a return to the old sources of power which had been deserted for the white man's gods. If it is true that the majority of the Kikuyu people are still, if anything, sitting on the Mau Mau side of the fence it is not wholly due to the terror inspired by the shock troops of Mau Mau. It is, in part, a religious determination to be quite sure that the old gods really are dead before they are finally deserted. That phenomenon is a common one in the history of all peoples when in a time of transition.

An event occurred in another part of East Africa fifty years ago which illustrates this same point and *might* afford a precedent for future developments in Kenya. In 1905 there took place, in what was then the German territory of Tanganyika, a rising known as the Maji-Maji rebellion. This embraced most of the tribes south of the Great Central Railway, more especially those living in the Rufiji valley and the area to the south of it. This could fairly be described as the 'last fling' of the old paganism, whatever promptings it may have received from external sources. The rebellion was suppressed with great ferocity. The significant fact is that in the sequel there sprang up a great demand for 'teachers' on the part of the very tribes which had been involved in the rebellion. Christian missions were able to respond to the demand, and through a network of schools they enabled large numbers of Africans to begin to make the transition to a new order of society. In the process large numbers became Christians.

The Maji-Maji rebellion and the Mau Mau in modern Kenya do not afford an exact parallel. But it is not unreasonable to believe that the demoralized Kikuyu people in Kenya may turn quite suddenly and in a spectacular way towards a Church which has been effectively reorganized round the surviving Confessors who formed the Christian resistance. It must be added, however, that if that is to happen the Church in

Kenya will have to concern itself intimately in the rebuilding of the social life of the people and that at every level. It can only hope to do this if resources in the way of men and women are put at its disposal by the Church in other parts of the world.

I have dwelt at some length on this particular illustration because I am convinced that far more understanding needs to be given to Africa if the Church is to discharge its obedience towards 'the healing of the nations'. The wounds of Africa are deep and the binding up of those wounds will need the kind of firm gentleness which is best experienced when it is combined with the skill of the trained healer. Lest anyone should think that the abnormalities of a single tribe lack a wider relevance and do not really contribute to our understanding of what is simmering in Africa, let me quote another brief paragraph from Dr. Carothers. He says:

'In general it would seem that all the elements of the vicious circle observed in Kikuyu country also occur in all other agricultural tribes of Kenya. They differ only in that the process has not gone so far. They are all, therefore, liable to the infection in varying degrees.'[1]

In saying that, Dr. Carothers limits himself to Kenya. Those who know their Africa would extend its relevance, at the very least, to the Zambesi and some would insist that its relevance holds as far as the Cape. It is most certainly relevant to Uganda. It would be a rash man who would presume to prophesy what can

[1] J. C. Carothers, op. cit., p. 20.

or cannot emerge out of the transition in which West Africa is involved.

At least we may claim to have established that in Asia and Africa we are confronted with a vast tearing up of human communities by their roots. Yet, in a way even this is a surface phenomenon which may distract our attention from something far more portentous. The path of a hurricane can be traced by uprooted trees and unroofed houses. The passage of an earthquake may only be discernible by seismographic instruments and its immediate effects may well be localized. But in the issue the result of an earthquake may be attended by far greater disaster than any arising from a hurricane. Just such a convulsion of the community of mankind, beginning with slight tremors and only here and there, as yet, reaching shock force, is to be discerned in the pace of population growth, at present far outstripping both the rate of food production and the ability to distribute what is produced. In Asia and Africa this pace of population growth presents one of the gravest threats to human life and to any kind of ordered society. I suggest to you that the under-swell in the ocean of man's life everywhere to-day, if I may change the metaphor, the unsettlement in all our human societies, can be traced back to a deep-seated, though as yet hardly articulate, fear of starvation.

Two quotations may serve to illuminate this danger and lead us on to our constructive task. An American scientist, Robert C. Cook, in a recent book on this subject, *Human Fertility: the Modern Dilemma*, cites, amongst other illustrations, that of Japan:

> 'Every square mile of arable land was called on to support 3,640 human beings—six people per acre. This is twelve times the population density of the United States. . . . Quite clearly, the most important determinant of the future of the Japanese people is this problem of population pressure.'[1]

After proposing some remedial measures he adds a mordant comment calculated to pose awkward questions for humanitarian consciences.

> 'Wiping out a series of communicable diseases in a population which does not have enough to eat, or bringing a torrent of new babies into an economy that cannot support even the people already born, are invitations to disaster.'[2]

My other illustration is from an advertisement for a system of mechanized farming with the dramatic title 'Hungry men have no ears' and beside it, a pair of hands filled with grain, held out towards a clamouring swarm of emaciated men and women. Under the title came these words:

> 'The millions of hungry men in the world have no ears for reason. They have only stomachs. Those who fill them will earn their life-long gratitude and allegiance— whatever their way of life. On our ability to grow sufficient cheap food, therefore, depends not only our way of life, but also the future of humanity.'

[1] *Human Fertility: the Modern Dilemma*, by Robert Cook, 1951, pp. 259–260.
[2] R. C. Cook, op. cit., p. 261.

When we have made every allowance for the rhetoric of an advertisement there remains, as we have seen, a disconcerting measure of truth in that analysis.

Uprooted men and women: millions who have broken with the traditions of their ancestors: the frustrated, the disillusioned, the fearful: the hungry: the pattering of millions of baby feet—there you have the circumstance within which the Church has to obey the imperative—go heal.

It may have seemed strange that a chapter on the ministry of healing should have come so far towards its close without any reference to a doctor or a nurse, to the medical missionary service of so many devoted Christians, without even a passing reference to a hospital or a clinic or a welfare centre. This has been quite deliberate. The fundamental sicknesses of men have always been sicknesses of the spirit and the mind. Never, perhaps, was this more obviously so than to-day. I have tried to establish the truth of this not only by referring you to the biblical view of man but also to the contemporary world. What I have tried to stress is reinforced by the witness of modern medicine itself in which the psycho-somatic approach is testimony that what most needs treatment is not the particular sickness but the sick person. Furthermore, to-day we know clearly that the sick person comes out of an environment that needs healing, an environment composed of people and of the land. Only a healing which makes a man whole and integrates him with his fellows in a true community, living in a right relation-

[81]

ship with God and with the good earth which God has given man, only such a healing is adequate to the imperative 'go heal'. For this reason the Church must not imagine that it can relegate the responsibilities of its healing mission to a representative company of physicians and nurses, surgeons and anæsthetists, pathologists and dispensers. These specialist workers are indispensable, but if their work is to be a healing work it cannot be done in isolation.

The *first* implication of this, if we may narrow our purview to the Christian Mission in Asia and Africa, is that the Christian hospital must be seen as an integral part of a common task in which Church and school and farm are seen, not as the possibly attractive agencies for the employment of those with no skill in healing, but as the actual points at which most of the healing is done, the front line of the attack on human need. To these, the real centres of healing, the hospital will be related as a source of inspiration, a school of technical knowledge, a resort for such cases as demand specialized skill, but not as being itself the centre of healing. If our understanding of healing has been correct, then the mission hospital needs to be understood as a unit in the healing community, the doctors and nurses as part of a team, the vast majority of whose members will never have walked the wards or been registered by the State as licensed to heal.

But if this calls for a change of outlook on the part of most Christian doctors and nurses, it also calls for as complete a change of view on the part of most clergy and teachers as well as of the Christian community as a whole. In practice this means that we have to work for the day when the local Christian community will recognize that the hospital is not either a foreign-owned and controlled extra to its life, still less a source of its own prestige and a place for the employment of local Christians, but is an essential part of that community's own witness of obedience to the command 'go heal'. That is the *second* implication of our understanding of the truth that healing is a work which cannot be done in isolation by the members of one skilled profession.

A *third* implication of this is the independence it affords the Church in its relation to the State. For a very long time the Church had an effective monopoly of scientific medicine in many parts of Asia and Africa. The awakening of the masses of these lands to the fact that technical resources to meet their physical needs are available: the achievement of political independence: a self-conscious nationalism: the emergence of the Social Service State: all these factors ensure that the days of monopoly are over. They also hasten the day when the large mission hospital will have to compete with a far better equipped hospital in its own neighbourhood run by the State. The day of the large mission hospital, with the possible exception of a few centres for training doctors or nurses, is nearly over. But a health-conscious community with its own medical unit, far from encroaching on the preserves or the prestige of the state medical service may well come to be viewed as a welcome ally.

A *fourth* implication is that a community which has

made healing in its fullest sense an integral element in its witness will have a new mobility for the communication of its gospel to the non-Christian world around. Here we may note the relevance of the biblical usage of the words *therapeia* and *latreuō* as we saw them in Revelation 22. Healing and worship have as their root meaning, service. A Church which goes out to serve the world around it will bring to that world healing, and it will bring the world to worship.

I have concentrated on some very practical implications of our understanding of the biblical meaning of healing, and of the contemporary situation. These implications are some of the ways in which the Church in its healing mission can at the local level demonstrate its ability to draw men and women to have a common purpose and so become in a true sense a community. These implications we have considered demand a mutual dependence, a mutual consideration, and a mutual helpfulness which ought to be the mark of the society of the divine forgiveness.

Here is a grass-root contribution to some of the global problems we have been considering. Let us be careful to start at the grass-roots. If we are faithful there we can be sure that the harvest will follow in God's good time. In a statement of a new medical policy relevant to our day published a few years ago by one of the English missionary societies, there occurred the following paragraph which is pertinent, especially when we are most likely to be overwhelmed by the dimensions of our task. It reads:

'The swarming millions are only abstractly regarded as such. They divide up into communities made up of family units, themselves made up of individuals whose ideals and efforts can make or mar the peace of the world. The whole gospel can permeate the communities of which those millions consist. With God's help we save lives, we try to make them more complete, because one obvious step in saving the world of men is to develop in individual men and women the vitality and ability to save their neighbours.'[1]

I have not forgotten the third biblical insight about the healing mission of the Church, that it presupposes a Church which is itself being healed. We rejoice, and rightly, in the development of the ecumenical movement of our day. We see in it a moving of the Spirit of God drawing the people of God into a unity from which a new power of healing may go out to the nations. But we dare not be complacent. A few indefatigable pioneers have stormed ahead, that is all as far as real adventure in unity is concerned—much talk and very little action. There are all too many evidences that the world can say, 'Physician, heal thyself' to a Church which is in no position to echo the answer which our Lord gave to the same challenge.[2]

I shall not soon forget how, at the Staten Island Conference of the International Missionary Council in July last year, I listened to an Asian leader speaking with prophetic intensity about the tragedy of Protestant disunity. He spoke of the invasion of Asia by

[1] *The Health of the Whole Man*, a Statement on C.M.S. Medical Policy, 1948, p. 8.
[2] Luke 4. 23 f.

new Christian sects. He was so bold as to characterize 'world-wide confessionalism' as a new menace to Christian unity. And in passing he told us of Japan where there are two thousand foreign missionaries, one thousand dedicated to co-operation and one thousand dedicated to non-co-operation, 'with', as he added, 'the "dedication" of the latter group being considerably more devoted than that of the former. Fifty-five new Christian sects have entered Japan since the War.'

On that rather sobering note I bring this lecture to an end, suggesting by way of epilogue that I hope I have provided you with material enough to enable you to say the Collect for St. Luke's Day with more than one special intention—

'Almighty God, who calledst Luke the Physician, whose praise is in the Gospel, to be an Evangelist and Physician of the soul: may it please thee, that, by the wholesome medicines of the doctrine delivered by him, all the diseases of our souls may be healed; through the merits of thy Son, Jesus Christ our Lord.'

IV

Go Baptize

WE have had our marching orders. These orders are 'to go into all the world', a geographical task in the first instance; 'to preach the gospel to every creature', which carries with it the acceptance of a continuing responsibility generation after generation; 'to cast out devils', that is to evangelize in depth, to deal with the sub-conscious and the un-conscious areas of revolt; 'to lay hands on the sick', that is to make men and women 'whole', to bear our witness to Him who said, 'I am come that they might have life and have it more abundantly'; 'to make disciples of all nations . . . teaching them to observe all things what-soever I have commanded you', a comprehensive task of education. Finally, integral to the whole of this many-sided activity is the command to 'baptize them in the Name of the Father, and of the Son and of the Holy Ghost', the restoration, that is, of all into the commonwealth of God, a commonwealth of which the Body of Christ, the Church, is the outward and visible promise and pledge.

[87]

Recent studies in the significance of Baptism for the Church of the New Testament, amongst them most notably the penetrating study of Professor Lampe, *The Seal of the Spirit*, make it clear beyond reasonable doubt that Christian Baptism finds its primary source of meaning in the Baptism of Christ Himself. That Baptism was at once 'the Baptism of John', and the long-awaited 'Baptism of the Spirit', and both were directly related to the fulfilment of the messianic hope. As Professor Lampe has it:

'Our Lord at His Baptism was designated the anointed Son whose mission of bringing in the new covenant of the Kingdom of God was to be worked out in terms of the Servant's task of intercession and of reconciliation through suffering.'[1]

The fulfilment of this task took place at Calvary: its proclamation beginning with the resurrection. This same anointing for Mission is then promised by the risen Christ to His disciples, and for our purpose it is particularly important to note that it was promised in the setting of the great commission. Here the Lucan narrative both in the Gospel[2] and in the Acts[3] supports by direct implication the imperative as recorded in St. Matthew.

The immediate practice of the apostolic Church, and Paul's profound doctrinal interpretation of that practice, are most readily explicable on the reckoning that they represent obedience to a divine instruction,

[1] *The Seal of the Spirit*, by G. W. H. Lampe, 1951, p. 38.
[2] Luke 24. 48–49.
[3] Acts 1. 8.

and reflection on the meaning of that obedience. To quote Professor Lampe again,

> 'Christ's own Baptism with the Old Testament background of the Servant prophecies, the Messianic unction with the Spirit, and the New Covenant, with, in addition, its anticipation . . . and symbolizing of the new relationship between God and man established through His saving work, is the ground and origin of Baptism as we find it practised in the apostolic Church, the sacrament of participation in the Spirit-anointing of the *Christos* through the response made by faith to His work of reconciliation. When, therefore, the completion of that work made it possible after Pentecost for believers to be baptized in the Name of Jesus Christ, the Baptism by which they were made partakers of the Christ corresponded in many respects to that which the Lord Himself received.'[1]

We may add that the correspondence was seen to involve not only the Baptism at the Jordan but also the Baptism at Golgotha. Cullmann in his study, *Baptism in the New Testament*, reminds us that,

> 'The parallelism between "being baptized" and "dying with Christ", whose origin goes back to the life of Jesus at his own Baptism by John in Jordan, is traceable through the whole of the New Testament and is not limited to Romans 6. 1 ff. We find it first in Paul himself in I Corinthians 1. 13, where Baptism is clearly conceived as participation in the Cross of Christ. "Was Paul crucified for you, or were ye baptized in the name of Paul?" Here the two expressions "you were baptized"

[1] G. W. H. Lampe, op. cit., p. 44.

and "another was crucified for you" are treated as synonymous.'

Before going on to try and understand the content of this parallelism, so fully developed by Paul in Romans, chapter 6, a word remains to be said about the association of the Trinitarian formula with the imperative 'go baptize'. Scholars may be right in disputing the probability of such a formula on the lips of Jesus. The early practice of the Church, on the evidence of the New Testament, would seem to support their judgment. The dispute remains, however, quite unimportant for our obedience to the imperative 'go baptize'. To baptize 'in the Name of Jesus' involves a great deal more than the mere English usage of the word 'Name' suggests. 'The Name' signifies the essential nature, the character, the power of Jesus. The witness of the New Testament is unequivocal that Jesus, in whose name the first Christians were baptized, was Lord, and that term, whether in Greek or Hebrew thinking, was unlimited in its range. Dr. Charles Lowry has surely made the most effective comment on the dispute by suggesting that by the time St. Matthew's Gospel was written, somewhere about A.D. 85,

'the believing and worshipping Church . . . looked in thanksgiving and trust and expectation to Three in the highest heaven—not simply to One. At the same time there was, they knew, a perfect unity of will, thought and action as among the Three . . . there was in this Trinity none of the personal dissonance, active spiritual divergence, and conflict of will, characteristic of the many Gods of paganism. And the idea of a single Divine name was retained. After all, the early Christians were, with few exceptions born Jews. If they were not sure about all the implications of the faith they had embraced in addition to that of the Synagogue, that is hardly a cause for surprise. It was not the first time that men have acted with courageous decision and found themselves in possession of a prize of rare and marvellous beauty, and yet have found themselves incompletely sure as to the reasons for their audacity.'[1]

Three centuries were to pass before a formula was to be arrived at which, in terms of Greek philosophy, would do as much justice to the revelation of God in Christian experience as any mere formula could hope to do. Long before St. Matthew had written his Gospel and incorporated the Trinitarian expansion of the Name of Jesus, Paul had claimed for Him 'the name which is above every name'.[2] That is the language of devotion. But, like all Paul's devotional language, it is implicitly Trinitarian. And we must assume that Paul had at his disposal the same resources of tradition as were later embodied in the Gospel narrative to describe what happened at the Baptism of Jesus. It is difficult on any reading of what is recorded in the Gospels not to find some awareness by the writers that for Jesus Himself, Baptism was what may not improperly be described as a Trinitarian experience. The Trinitarian formula in St. Matthew is not an 'invention' of St. Matthew, however much we may believe it

[1] *The Trinity and Christian Devotion*, by Charles W. Lowry, 1946, pp. 56–57.
[2] Phil. 2. 9.

to be an interpretation of what Jesus implied when He gave His command 'Go baptize'.

The word 'to baptize' has as its primary meaning 'to submerge in water' and for its object, be it person or thing, it denotes to 'go under', to be overwhelmed. By a strict analogy in the realm of understanding the word overwhelm suggests being 'out of one's depth'. So it was with

> 'Stout Cortez when, with eagle eyes,
> He stared at the Pacific, and all his men
> Looked at each other with a wild surmise,
> Silent, upon a peak in Darien.'[1]

The poet is describing men 'overwhelmed' by their discovery, awed by the majesty of what they see, by no means fully aware of what it signifies. In so describing them he is, of course, describing his own feelings as he first dips into those 'realms of gold' represented by classical literature. What Keats describes is in transcendent measure what we find in the New Testament as being involved in the experience of Baptism. The 'going under' the water is the symbolic act which corresponds to the overwhelming of the mind and soul of the one who is baptized. This sense of being spiritually overwhelmed may precede Baptism or it may follow Baptism but in the New Testament it is certainly associated with it. It is a sense of being 'out of one's depth' in relation to what God has done. For one man this may be induced by

[1] *On Looking into Chapman's Homer*, Keats.

a vision of the holiness of God and the man's own
sinfulness: for another it may be the wonder of the
love of God which meets the sinner in judgment and
mercy so that the baptized can see his sin and all its
consequences 'overwhelmed' in the love of God: for
yet a third it may well appear as a dying with his sin
and being brought to life again without the sin, a new
creature. Always when we consider Baptism in the
New Testament we have to see it under some form of
an overwhelming experience through which the individual passes, symbolically in his body, mentally
and spiritually in the full range of his personality.
Only by such associations can we begin our
appreciation of the lyrical notes of New Testament
Christianity.

Remembering that in the early centuries Lent was
primarily concerned with preparation for Baptism, the
solemn occasion of which was immediately before the
Easter Eucharist, itself celebrated at midnight, we
can see the traditional appropriateness in our Liturgy
of the Collect for Easter Eve and the Epistle for
Easter Day. That collect, a vigil prayer, reads:

> 'Grant, O Lord, that as we are baptized into the death
> of thy blessed Son, our Saviour Jesus Christ, so by con-
> tinual mortifying our corrupt affections we may be
> buried with him; and that through the grave, and gate
> of death, we may pass to our joyful resurrection; for his
> merits, who died, and was buried, and rose again for us,
> thy Son Jesus Christ our Lord.'

That that Collect has a baptismal reference in its
primary intention would seem to be suggested by the

Easter Lection, itself, from the earliest times of which we have record, part of the first Eucharist of the newly baptized, which begins with the words:

'If ye then be risen with Christ, seek those things which are above, where Christ sitteth on the right hand of God. Set your affection on things above, not on things on the earth: For ye are dead, and your life is hid with Christ in God.'[1]

But, as yet, we have only touched the fringe of what Baptism in the New Testament signifies. The lyrical note to which we have referred is part of the song of the redeemed, who have been delivered by God from the separations caused by sin, and who now know that an atonement has taken place, not only by the testimony of the Spirit in their hearts assuring them of peace with God, but by the actual experience of that fellowship into which they enter as they come up out of the waters of Baptism.

'In Baptism', says Cullmann, '. . . the individual is, for the first time and once for all, set at the point of history where salvation operates—where even now, in the interval between the resurrection and the Second Coming, the death and resurrection of Christ, the forgiveness of sins and the Holy Ghost, are according to God's will to be efficacious for Him.'[2]

This place in history is the Church, the fellowship of those who have been grafted into the one Body. Lampe has an attractive rendering of I Corinthians

[1] Col. 3. 1–3, A.V. and P.B.V.
[2] Cullmann, op. cit., p. 30.

12. 13, in which he suggests that Paul is here picking up a favourite Old Testament metaphor of fresh water irrigating the desert. His rendering reads:

'For in one Spirit were we all baptized unto one body, whether Jews or Greeks, whether slaves or freedmen, and were all "watered" with one Spirit.'[1]

Something of the thrill of the life in this new fellowship into which Baptism ushers the Christian, Paul describes in his words to the Colossians[2] which Lightfoot paraphrases to read:

'We were slaves in the land of darkness. God rescued us from this thraldom. He transplanted us thence, and settled us as free colonists and citizens in the Kingdom of His Son, in the realms of light.'[3]

These words, indeed, may serve to take us yet further into the significance of Baptism for the New Testament. Paul's words to the Colossians just cited are surely an echo of words he had once heard from the Lord Himself on the Damascus road. As we read them we will not fail to notice the setting of Paul's own missionary imperative. In Acts 26 we hear him telling King Agrippa of how he had once, years before, been arrested by a voice. Replying to the challenge he said, 'Who are you, Lord?'

'And the Lord said, "I am Jesus whom you are persecuting. But rise and stand upon your feet; for I have

---

[1] G. W. H. Lampe, op. cit., p. 56.
[2] Col. 1. 12 and 13.
[3] *The Epistles of St. Paul—Colossians and Philemon*, by J. B. Lightfoot, 1880, p. 141.

appeared to you for this purpose, to appoint you to
serve and bear witness to the things in which you have
seen me and to those in which I will appear to you,
delivering you from the people and from the Gentiles—
to whom I send you to open their eyes, that they may
turn from darkness to light and from the power of
Satan to God, that they may receive forgiveness of sins
and a place among those who are sanctified by faith
in me." '[1]

We note in that passage the same sense of a great
deliverance as we find in Colossians, of a transfer from
darkness to light, of life in a new community.

This thought of a transfer of whole peoples to a new
allegiance as a sequel to a decisive victory seems to
suggest one of the most important aspects under which
we are to conceive of our imperative 'go baptize' in the
light of the relationship of Christian Baptism to the
Baptism of our Lord. Here I believe that Cullmann
offers us a clue which is of the very greatest significance. I would ask leave to quote from him at some
length.

'For an understanding of the deeper meaning of the
Baptism of Jesus', he writes, 'it is significant that Jesus
at the very moment when he is baptized hears this
voice, which offers him . . . the title of that Son who will
fulfil the Mission which in the Old Testament is pro-
phetically ascribed to the suffering Servant of God.'
'Here we find the answer to the question', continues
Cullmann, 'What meaning has Baptism to the forgiveness of sins for Jesus himself in the New Testament?
At the moment of his Baptism he receives the com-

[1] Acts 26. 15–18.

mission to undertake the role of the suffering Servant of God, who takes on himself the sins of his people. Other Jews came to Jordan to be baptized by John for their *own* sins. Jesus, on the contrary, at the very moment when he is baptized like other people hears a voice which fundamentally declares: *Thou* art baptized not for *thine own* sins but for those of the whole people. For thou art he of whom Isaiah prophesied, that he must suffer representatively for the sins of the people. This means that Jesus is baptized in view of his death, which effects forgiveness of sins for all men. For this reason Jesus must unite himself in solidarity with his whole people, and go down himself to Jordan, that "all righteousness may be fulfilled".

'In this way, Jesus' answer to the Baptist "to fulfil all righteousness" ("*plerōsai pasan dikaiosunen*" Matt. 3. 15), acquires a precise meaning. The Baptism of Jesus is related to *dikaiosune*, not only his own but also that of the whole people. The word *pasan* is probably to be underlined here. Jesus' reply, which exegetes have always found difficult to explain, acquires a concrete meaning: Jesus will effect a general forgiveness. Luke (like Mark) does not use this word, but he emphasizes in his own way the same fact at 3. 21: "Now when *all* the people were baptized (*lapanta ton laon*), Jesus also was baptized". It is clear, in view of the voice from heaven, why Jesus must conduct himself like other people. He is distinguished from the mass of other baptized people, who are baptized for their own sins, as the One called to the office of the Servant of God who suffers *for all others.*'

Cullmann then points his conclusion:

'Thus the Baptism of Jesus points forward to the end, to the climax of his life, the Cross, in which alone all Baptism will find its fulfilment. There Jesus will achieve a general Baptism. In his own Baptism in Jordan he received commission to do this.'[1]

The importance of that interpretation of Cullmann for our consideration of the divine imperative 'go baptize' lies in the fact that it links Baptism with a decisive act of God which was universal in its relevance. The dominion of evil over individual men was overthrown, a victory in the life of the individual which we have already seen to be represented in the Baptism of each Christian. But more than this, in Christ's Baptism for all men at Golgotha the dominion of evil over all men was, in fact, overthrown. The 'Mission to the Gentiles'[2] is explicitly defined as opening men's eyes to that fact, to show them that Satan's usurped dominion is at an end. At the Cross God did something in Christ, in relation to the powers of evil, which Paul can describe with the words

'He disarmed the principalities and powers and made a public example of them, triumphing over them in him.'[3]

Even more important still we have to see that, according to the New Testament, something was achieved 'in Christ' which transcends the totality of the human race and lifts the eyes to the vision of a universe restored. When in Ephesians we read of God's

'purpose which he set forth in Christ as a plan for the

[1] Cullmann, op. cit., pp. 18–19.
[2] Acts 26. 18.
[3] Col. 2. 15.

fulness of time, to unite all things in him, things in heaven and things on earth',[1]

we see God bringing together again a dislocated universe, of man and things, with Christ as their universal bond. This is but to say, in other words, what Paul says in his letter to the Romans that

'the creation itself will be set free from its bondage to decay and obtain the glorious liberty of the children of God'.[2]

In thus emphasizing the universality of what was achieved at Calvary, when the whole world was baptized; in insisting that the New Testament sees even greater depths in that mystery, I am concerned that we should recognize that our own Baptism, as Christians, is not simply into the Body of Christ, conceived as that part of mankind which has been saved. Our Baptism is into the Body of Christ which exists as the nucleus of a redeemed humanity, nay more, of a redeemed cosmic order. And, as that nucleus, it exists to proclaim the divine victory and to insist on the Crown Rights of the Redeemer over all His dominion. The Church is not the *regnum Christi*, it is rather a brotherhood of expectancy whose expectation takes the form of an active obedience to the missionary imperative.

As we thus understand the Baptism which Christ underwent at Calvary and the relation of our Baptism to it we are rescued from any paltry understanding of

[1] Eph. 1. 10.
[2] Rom. 8. 21.

[99]

salvation. To have been 'buried with him by baptism',[1] to have been overwhelmed in the flood which overwhelmed Him, is to know ourselves at one with Him in His attitude to the world for which He died. To 'walk in newness of life',[2] having been raised from the dead by the same power which raised Him, is to have been initiated into the mystery of that plan whereby all things, as well as all people, are to be 'united in Him'.[3] To be baptized, then, is to share in the divine victory. And this victory is a victory won in the real world of men and things.

In that real world the forces of sin and death and the devil, all that are corruptions and make for corruption, exercise a fatal sway over the minds and hearts of men, whose eyes are blinded to the victory of Christ. The mission of the Church is to open the eyes of the blind and demonstrate the victory already won. That is the logical conclusion to which our whole argument has led us.

Holding the steps which have led us to this point firmly in mind—Christ's Baptism as the norm of our Baptism: the fulfilment of Christ's Baptism in Calvary: the scope of that Baptism as being for all mankind and all the universe: the deliverance which we have found through Christ's Baptism being made operative in our Baptism: the new life of co-operation with God's universal plan to which our Baptism com-

[1] Rom. 6. 4.
[2] Ibid.
[3] Eph. 1. 10.

mits us—we must go on to claim that there is a legitimate sense in which we can speak of baptizing all our relationships into Christ. If Christ died for all men then the Baptism of His death bears directly upon the relationships of all men. For man as we know him is never man-in-isolation, but always man-in-relationship, right or wrong, with God, his fellow-men, and the world of nature around him. We can then properly speak of the Church's Mission as being to 'take every thought captive to obey Christ',[1] to refuse to allow the reign of disobedience to continue unchallenged. From here we can see how natural and inevitable it is for the Christian to seek to transform society until it in turn reflects the glory of God. It is in conformity with these insights that we can speak of a Christian society, a Christian culture, a Christian civilization, and seek by God's help to make the society, the culture and the civilization in which we live more Christian.

The New Testament shows this actually happening wherever the baptized life is being lived by those whose 'faith *is* working through love'.[2] This is, in large part, the force of Paul's argument and appeal in Galatians 5. 'Walking by the Spirit' is for Paul no abnormal ecstatic experience. It is the only proper corollary of Baptism[3] as we have already seen. And the 'walking' takes place in the homes and market places of actual communities in which the Christian has to share in the business and civic life. We know

[1] II Cor. 10. 5.
[2] Gal. 5. 6.
[3] I Cor. 12. 13.

[101]

what that local setting was in New Testament times. Whether or not Ramsay is wholly justified in his commentary on Galatians 5. 19–21, when he breaks down the 'sins of the flesh' there enumerated into the typical evils current in Anatolia at that time, is neither here nor there. But there certainly are contemporary human societies a-plenty in which, under crude or sophisticated forms, we find a popular religion which condones 'immorality, impurity, licentiousness, idolatry and sorcery'. We do not have to go to Anatolia to see municipal life corrupted by 'enmity, strife, jealousy, anger and selfishness'. 'Dissension, party-spirit, envy, drunkenness, carousing and the like' disfigure sections of society in every country in the world in our own day, as surely as in the days of Paul.

Into just such a welter of perversity men and women who had been 'baptized into Christ'[1] came in the first century and there, in that setting, demonstrated that it is possible 'in the flesh' to live a life of faithful obedience to Christ.[2] Paul never confused man's animal nature with the perversion of that nature under the influence of sin. Indeed for him not the least part of the glory of the gospel was that it liberated man's animal nature from the dominion of sin so that, in fact, the flesh itself is the redeemed sphere in which the liberty of Christ is enjoyed. It is 'in the flesh', precisely there, but now baptized into Christ, that in the Anatolian cities of the first century, and in how

[1] Gal. 3. 27.
[2] Gal. 2. 20.

many more in Asia and Africa, in Europe and America, down the centuries and to-day, men and women have walked 'in the Spirit', proving the victory of Christ over all that perverted their humanity.

This took demonstrable shape in a life of quite new relationships in which love, joy, peace, were the very constituents of the Christian Eucharist, the heart of a new relationship with God. No less demonstrable was the new sense of responsibility in the common life which was introduced by men who knew the secrets of patience, kindness and sheer goodness. Social life, whether public or domestic, was transfigured by a new conception of faithfulness, of gentleness and of self-control.

All that was happening in Anatolia in the fourth decade of the first century; that is evident from St. Paul's letter to the Galatians. In that letter we do well to remember he is not propagating a new idea so much as appealing to a proved experience which he and his readers had in common. He was appealing to their Baptism and to the testimony of the deliverance which that had worked.

Let us briefly consider two of the infinite variety of relationships which make up human life, and see how in our own day they are being baptized into Christ. The first is a relationship between persons, the second is a relationship between persons and things.

In that same letter to the Galatians Paul made one of the most far-reaching of all his claims for Baptism when he wrote:

'For as many of you as were baptized into Christ have put on Christ. There is neither Jew nor Greek, there is neither slave nor free, there is neither male nor female; for you are all one in Christ Jesus.'

The trouble about the Jew and the Greek was that they found it so difficult ever to meet. The spiritual pride of the one and the intellectual pride of the other set up barriers between them which have only been broken down, where they have been broken down, through Christ. The meeting of Jew and Greek in Christ produced the classical Christian culture of the Middle Ages and still inspires the profoundest spiritual insights of the West.

In Christ there is neither slave nor free. Slowly, very slowly, the conviction that all men are 'one in Christ' has had its effect upon the political, economic and social organization of society. The rights of man, or some of them, have even found their way into the heart of a nation's history as you have reason to know well, for do you not claim some of them as being 'self-evident propositions'? In our day we have seen an attempt made to establish a Declaration of Human Rights which would be valid for all men everywhere. Trace that idea back and we find ourselves at Calvary. All men have rights because Christ died for all men. But there was nothing self-evident about that when Paul was drawing out the implications of Calvary for the Galatians who had been baptized.

But of these new relationships which follow upon Baptism the one to which I want most to draw your attention is that between men and women. When Paul wrote that in Christ there was 'neither male nor female' he did not mean that sex had been abolished or that it had been sublimated. What he did mean was that in Christ the old order of antagonism, of exploitation, of injustice had been done away and replaced by 'the true pattern of sexual relation—man and woman living and working in real partnership, and thus exhibiting a renewal of that belongingness in which and for which they were created'.[1] The circumstances of his time did not allow Paul to develop this conception of partnership between man and wife. Indeed, those very circumstances, the position of woman in ancient society and the revolutionary implications of being 'in Christ' compelled him to legislate with a caution that has unhappily influenced the whole of subsequent history. Yet even within the limits set by the contemporary scene Paul set out to regulate the relations within Christian marriage on the basis of Christ's love for the Church. Baptism, as we have seen, was regulative for that analogy. In Baptism the Christian became a new creature. As Paul has it in writing to the Colossians:

'You have put off the old nature with its practices and have put on the new nature, which is being renewed in knowledge after the image of its Creator.'[2]

Dr. Sherwin Bailey in a recent article in the English journal, *Theology*, quotes that passage and puts the

[1] *Woman and the Church's Lay Ministry*, by Sherwin Bailey, *Theology*, No. 411, September 1954, p. 326.
[2] Col. 3. 10.

word *image* in italics in reference to an earlier observation that, in the first chapter of Genesis, male and female are created simultaneously as an *Imago Dei*.[1] In that extremely able article he makes a further point with reference to the analogy of Christ's love for the Church as the pattern of Christian marriage. After suggesting that the thought of the Heavenly Bridegroom and the Bride was well-fitted to Paul's purpose of bringing sanctity into the existing pattern of relationships without prematurely overthrowing them, he adds:

'But the analogy is independent of any particular social pattern; its enduring basis is the fact that the *henosis* of Christ and the Church is reproduced in the *henosis* of the "one flesh", and that in each case the relation is constituted and maintained by a mutual love of unique quality. The subordination *motif* is accidental and not intrinsic to the Christian theology of marriage.'[2]

Certain, at least, it is that all down the centuries we can discern the outworking of this new relationship in the characteristic achievement of the Christian home and the Christian family relationship. While in the flesh, countless ordinary men and women have learnt to walk together in the Spirit. That achievement, that Baptism of domestic life lies at the base of the whole stability of the western way of life. I have been struck and deeply moved by the frequency and unanimity of the statement made by Asians and Africans that for

[1] Gen. 1. 27.
[2] Sherwin Bailey, op. cit., p. 325.

them the best thing they have met in the West has been the Christian home. Recently I heard of a young Muslim student who had been converted to Christ and who, being asked what had led to this decision, replied that, in a Christian home which he had visited, he had for the first time in his life seen the pattern of how a husband should treat a wife. He spoke as a former Muslim man. I have no doubt that, with a deeper awareness of what the Baptism of a home can mean, he would have recognized as equally remarkable how that Christian wife treated her husband.

I might go on from this relationship to consider that astonishing Baptism of relationship which makes it possible for a man and a woman 'in Christ' to be friends outside marriage and for the inescapable sexual element in that relationship to be genuinely sublimated. This is one way of describing the freedom of women in our western world, a freedom which derives directly from the insight of Galatians 3. 28 read in the light of Calvary. You do not find that freedom where Christ is not known and where His imperative 'go baptize' has not yet been obeyed.

But there is another aspect of this relationship of men and women which I would commend to your attention as being of great importance to the Christian Mission in Asia and Africa. It involves a direct application of the principle of Galatians 3. 28 in the sphere of education.

In an earlier chapter I have referred to the peculiar disruptions at work in East Africa. In doing so I quoted Dr. Carothers as having defined the basic problem as lying in the fact that African society is in a process of violent transition. Writing then, in particular, of the Kikuyu, he says:

'Educational diversity within the tribe is now most strikingly exemplified in a gross disparity in the levels of advancement of the men and women. With many notable exceptions, the women on the whole lag far behind . . . the extreme diversity of advancement in different sectors of Kikuyu society, and especially the diversity between the men and women, is the most striking and unfortunate feature of transition in Kikuyuland. Where all move on together, transition could be easier; but here the problem of transition becomes a different one for men and women.'[1]

He then goes on to show how, all over the Kikuyu country, the last twenty-five years has seen a breakdown of the old traditional patterns of tribal and family cohesion. To a considerable extent the Kikuyu woman has succeeded in maintaining the old ways and many of the old beliefs which she has tried to transmit to her children. But she has lost her men folk, sometimes literally and altogether, more often for varying periods of separation while he works in the town and she in the family home. He goes away and learns new ideas. She cherishes the old ones and fears the new. He worships at strange altars. She serves the household gods.

All this means an inner conflict between the man and the woman which disrupts the home still further.

[1] J. C. Carothers, op. cit., p. 9.

There is here no conceivable basis for the Christian idea of a home which is built on a genuine partnership. Not for the African, such as here described, is there

'the joy of going through life hand in hand with the comrade of one's choice, sharing one another's burdens, stimulating one another's courage, doubling one another's sagacity, buckling on one another's armour, wearing one another's laurels, and easing one another's pain.'[1]

That conception of marriage depends upon the Baptism referred to in Galatians 3. 27–28. The most urgent need in Kenya, as in most of Africa and of Asia to-day, is to press forward with the Christian education of girls and women. Only so can we, in practice, obey the divine imperative 'go baptize' in such a way as to relate it to races in transition.

Let me briefly refer to another relationship which needs to be baptized, a relationship between man and things. An African headmaster, not long ago, wrote to thank a friend of mine for a course of talks he had given in that African school. In the letter occurred this sentence:

'We greatly appreciated your helpful talks on the application of the teaching of Jesus Christ in our agricultural work and hygiene, as well as in spiritual things. Until now we regarded agriculture and hygiene as merely secular subjects, without any connexion with Christianity.'

[1] *Race Problems in the New Africa*, by W. C. Willoughby, 1923, p. 104.

In how many schools, and not only in Africa, are there boys and girls waiting to make the discovery that there are no merely secular subjects without any relation to Christianity? But suppose children go through their schooling and this is never pointed out to them. Suppose the Scripture lesson is never seen in the context of the other subjects, and suppose each of the other subjects to be treated as 'a whole by itself'. Then according to taste, one with a bias towards curiosity will make biological research his 'knowledge'; another will want to 'make things' and will welcome the precise disciplines of mathematics; and so on. Can it be wondered at that 'agriculture and hygiene' and all other studies are regarded as 'merely secular subjects, without any connexion with Christianity'? By such an artificial division we have denied that all the world and everything in it are 'all parts of His dominion'. We have refused to assert 'the Crown Rights of the Redeemer' over all parts of His world. We have failed to bear witness to the gospel, we have failed in obedience to our orders.

Yet 'we are ambassadors for Christ, God making his appeal through us. We beseech you on behalf of Christ, be reconciled to God.'[1]

Is our persuasion of men to enter the commonwealth of God, to be reinstated as partners with Him in His universe, a divine beseeching at all worthy of Him by whom *all* things exist? That is a very searching question. Witnessing to the gospel through school and hospital, through welfare centre and clinic, through

[1] II Cor. 5. 20.

rural development and community service of every kind here finds its justification or it cannot be justified at all.

As fellow-workers with the God who made the world we refuse to call anything 'common or unclean', and dismiss it therefore as beneath our attention or beyond the redeeming grace of God. As fellow-workers with God we insist that our Gospel bears directly on every aspect of man's life, individual and social. Our objective is nothing less than a universe redeemed, and we dare to be so ambitious because we believe with St. Paul, in the same sense and with the same humility as his, that in this matter 'we have the mind of Christ'.

For all these reasons I believe we can claim that the African schoolmaster who listened to that missionary applying 'the teaching of Jesus Christ in our agricultural work and hygiene' may have been hearing the gospel preached for the first time at a level which really affected his life. I do not know if that was the case, but it may have been so, as in many other cases it certainly has been. For the gospel of the saving grace of God comes alive for a man when he sees himself to be a rebel against God and needing above all else pardon and reinstatement. And the way in which a man treats God's good earth may be as much a mark of the way in which he is a rebel against God as the way he treats his wife. Marriage can be legalized rape and so can farming. The abuse of the acquisitive instinct, no less than the abuse of the sex instinct, demands repentance, that turning of the whole person

[111]

in a new direction which it is the object of the gospel to secure. The Lord Christ once likened His Kingdom to 'a grain of mustard seed, which a man took, and cast into his garden'. The phenomenal growth of the tree which sprang from that mustard seed argued soil sufficient for deep rooting. Maybe we have thought so much of the seed that we have forgotten the soil into which it is thrown. Perhaps we might exercise our imaginations on the thought that 'in the place where He was crucified there was a garden' and that His eyes looked down from the Cross upon the tragedy of soil-erosion as well as of soul-erosion and that His death had something to do with both. We Christians need to beware of taking too limited a view of sin and too restricted a view of grace, lest we find ourselves regarding 'agriculture and hygiene as merely secular subjects, without any connexion with Christianity'. This is only a modern form of one of the oldest and deadliest of the heresies which have turned men from the truth of God—the heresy that a man's soul and a man's body are separate and opposed entities and that salvation is the escape of the soul from the body.

In these two very practical illustrations from the world of our day I have tried to show what it means when the Baptism of Calvary, working its way down through the Baptism of the Christian and his incorporation thereby into the Body of Christ, impinges upon the work-a-day world. We can see in these two illustrations a little of what is really meant by Paul when he writes:

'If anyone is in Christ he is a new creation; the old has passed away, behold, the new has come. All this is from God, who through Christ reconciled us to himself and gave us the ministry of reconciliation.'[1]

Perhaps we can also glimpse the limitless ranges in which Christ's victory can be demonstrated once we take seriously the imperative 'go baptize'.

[1] II Cor. 5. 17–18.

V

The 'How' of Obedience

IN the Gospels, as in the Acts, the Imperative is, for
the Christian, no arbitrary command, no authori-
tarian decree addressed as from a distance to the one
who is commanded, as impersonal as it is remote.
Involved in the command is the assurance of the
enabling and continuing presence of the One who commands. 'Lo, I am with you always'[1] becomes an experienced fact when the One who commands sends the
promise of the Father upon His disciples and they
receive the Holy Spirit.[2] That is the underlying reality
which transforms an imperative into an inspiration.
So Paul, pressed beyond measure in the pursuit of his
obedience, gravely embarrassed by 'a thorn in the
flesh' which seems to frustrate his ability to give an
obedience that is worthy, prays for deliverance. The
prayer is answered by the transfiguration of the embarrassment—'but he said unto me "My grace is
sufficient for you, for my power is made perfect in
weakness" '. And Paul rejoins 'I will all the more

[1] Matt. 28. 20.
[2] Luke 24. 49; Acts 1. 8.

[114]

gladly boast of my weaknesses, that the power of Christ may rest upon me. For the sake of Christ, then, I am content with weakness, insults, hardships, persecutions and calamities; for when I am weak, then I am strong.'[1]

In turn, that discovery of Paul reminds us that the enabling and continuing Presence is always to the end an infinitely demanding Presence. There is no discharge from the commission. He who hears the command 'to go', and obeys, enlists for life. The very frustrations of his obedience which he finds within himself are an incentive not an excuse. The obstacles which circumstances present to the fulfilment of his mission prove to be opportunities. Writing to the Christians at Philippi, himself chained to a Roman soldier, Paul can say 'I want you to know, brethren, that what has happened to me has really served to advance the gospel, so that it has become known throughout the whole Prætorian guard and to all the rest that my imprisonment is for Christ.'[2] The man who has got beyond frustration, who can see in the malice of false friends that even they and their malice are caught up into the Imperative and its outworking, and who can say then 'I rejoice. Yes, and I shall rejoice',[3] is entitled to say, without being accused of hyperbole, 'I can do all things in him who strengthens me',[4] because he knows, having proved, that

---

[1] II Cor. 12. 8–10.
[2] Phil. 1. 12–13.
[3] Phil. 1. 18–19.
[4] Phil. 4. 13.

'absolute demand' is always accompanied by 'final succour'.

In thus understanding the sequel to obedience we recognize that what finally characterizes it is the assimilation of the one who obeys to the One who both commands and accompanies, so that there is a sharing of a common mind and will. It is this which Paul points to when, having expounded the wonder of the mind of Christ and His will for man's salvation, he can go on, as one who has felt the divine constraint, to say that for himself his discipleship is a response to a demand to share his Lord's sufferings, 'because Christ Jesus has made me his own.'[1]

The Christian imperative, then, is never just a compliance with an order, going to preach because we have been ordered to preach, to teach, to heal, to baptize as routine responses to an imperative just because it is Christ who issues it. That is never how the New Testament understands the Mission either of the disciple or of the Church. Always it is something far more intimate, and infinitely more demanding. From Paul again we can discover something of all that is involved in obedience if we study the pictures which he paints for us in I Corinthians 13. First there is the picture of the disciple whose obedience is essentially compliance with an order. There is no warmth in it because love has not been engaged. Duty is performed impersonally both in relation to the One who commands and in relation to those towards whom the service is rendered. The first three verses paint in

[1] Phil. 3. 10, 12.

[116]

matchless imagery the essential lovelessness of all fanaticism, of all self-chosen martyrdom, of all essentially self-centred discipleship. It is no accident that it is the 'I' of the disciple which holds the centre of the picture.

Then comes the portrait of the Christ Himself, an objective study of Love as the inspiring source of service, epitomized in the Servant who is the Master.

Finally we have another picture of the disciple. No longer is he a dominating figure, self-assertive, thrusting. Instead we see him caught up into a likeness of his Lord so that for him too 'Love never ends'. And the things he does for love are for the disciple only the means, never the ends. The ends are beyond his sight. He can only see through a glass darkly but he knows that Love must win and so he obeys in love.

We may imagine these three pictures as forming a triptych. The centre-piece is the portrait of the Christ who is Love. In the segment which faces us on the left we see that the disciple is looking away from Christ, preoccupied with his own employment as a disciple, self-absorbed. In the other, the disciple is looking towards Christ and something of the radiance of Christ is already reflected on the face of the disciple.

It is under such a form that Paul would teach us that obedience to the imperatives 'go preach', 'go teach', 'go heal', 'go baptize', can only be fulfilled as we recognize that embracing them all, the inner meaning of each, is the far more searching imperative, 'go love'.

A Christian is a man who stands under that im-

perative and finds in that imperative both the interpretation of, and the inspiration for, the particular
service to which he is called and for which he is
equipped.

Perhaps the time has come to make explicit what,
I hope, has all along been implicit and clear, that in
considering these imperatives we have been thinking
of the commission given by Christ to His Church, a
commission which can only be fulfilled by the Church
as a whole. Each member of the Church stands under
the divine imperative whatever the particular manner
in which he is called to obey it. Some words of Dr.
Oldham in his book *Life is Commitment* have a direct
bearing on the Christian and his discipleship—

'There are some things in life', says Dr. Oldham, 'and
they may be the most important things—that we cannot know by research or reflection, but only by com-
mitting ourselves. We must dare in order to know. We
may find ourselves confronted with a demand about
which we know that, if we respond to it, the gates of
life remain open to us, while if we refuse it we shall be
condemned to live henceforward on a lower level. To
live means that we are not merely observers, investi-
gators, technicians but that we have at times to stake
our whole existence, and it is only by making these
great and daring commitments that we can experience
and know what life really is.'[1]

Such a demand and such a commitment are involved
in Christ's personal word to each and everyone who
would be a disciple—'Follow me'.

[1] J. H. Oldham, op. cit., p. 24.

That demand, matched by a response of obedience, opens to the disciple all the inspiration and enablement for service which we have considered. There will be 'varieties of service'[1] and of working between those who are called to apostleship and prophecy and who may have to go to the ends of the earth, and others who as 'helpers' and 'administrators'[2] do the backroom jobs of the Church's Mission, and who do not go to distant places. The latter, whether as prayer-partners or as typists, make the work of the former possible. Both share the same resources of power. This needs to be understood as fundamental to any true understanding of the Church and of 'how' its obedience to the divine imperative is discharged. Paul's whole argument in I Corinthians 12 is based on the analogy of the human body whose several parts belong together so essentially that it is impossible for one member to say of another 'I have no need of you'. Elsewhere, using the same analogy, he sees 'the whole body, joined and knit together by every joint with which it is supplied, when each part is working properly, makes bodily growth and upbuilds itself in love.'[3] The recognition of that fundamental fact about the structure of relationships within the Church is indispensable if the Mission of the Church is to be seen in its due proportions.

Having established this principle that without respect of persons God gives His grace to enable every disciple for his or her particular obedience, we can go

[1] I Cor. 12. 5.   [2] I Cor. 12. 28.
[3] Eph. 4. 16.

on to recognize one essential note about the Mission
of the Church as we find it recorded both in Scripture
and in history. This essential note is provided by the
pilgrim character of the Church. Notwithstanding all
its obligation towards the redemption of the particular
locality in which it finds itself, each component part
of the Church has a wider obligation. In imagination,
in prayer, in offering and in service, the local church
knows itself as part of the whole Church, obeys as part
of the whole Church, in so far as it sees its Mission as
extending 'to the end of the earth'. It is a deep
Christian instinct which inspired the writer of the
Epistle to the Hebrews to say 'here we have no lasting
city, but we seek the city which is to come.'[1] The
command 'go' echoes in the ears of the Christian
disciple with an insistence which cannot be denied.
There is always much more land to be possessed for
God. There are always teeming multitudes of those
who have not so much as heard of the gospel of the
love of God. There are always new areas of human life
to which the gospel has to be applied. History is a
dynamic process. It is never static. The Christian is
continually faced with new developments in the pattern of social life with which he has to be concerned,
with new concentrations of power which have to be
tamed, with new relationships which have to be sanctified. The Christian stands always under the imperative to go—preach, teach, heal, baptize, however new
the forms under which that imperative has to be
obeyed.

[1] Heb. 13. 14.

This going forth of obedience, because it is a sending forth by the Lord, is properly called 'Mission' and he who is sent forth is properly called a 'missionary'. The word 'missionary' needs to be understood and interpreted but it must not be discarded.

In understanding the word missionary our first task is to make an elementary but very necessary distinction. Because every Christian is called to share in the Mission of the Church, then any Christian who commits himself to the Mission is in a true and vital sense a missionary. This sense of mission within the local framework is, and ought to be, an abiding source of inspiration for the Christian whose service is looked for 'at-home'. For convenience sake, however, the term 'missionary' is very reasonably confined to the Christian who is sent from home to serve 'abroad'. There is no qualitative distinction between the one who is told to stay and the one who is told to go. Both are obeying a divine imperative, if they are being obedient at all. But just as a business firm has a headquarters staff and travellers, and the two are not confused, being necessary to each other, yet distinct, so the Church, by giving the title 'missionary' to its travellers, makes a distinction when there is an obvious difference.

If that difference is allowed it remains to be noted that 'abroad' does not of necessity carry a geographical reference, though it most commonly does so. Much depends on the locality in which the Church is set which is sending out missionaries. In the history of the United States, for instance, it is true to say that the

greater part of its missionary energy in the nineteenth
century, and far the greater number of its missionaries, found full scope within the borders of the conti-
nental United States. Again, in the Church of South
India to-day it would be unreal to suggest that their
representatives in New Guinea were more entitled to
the description 'missionary' than their workers among
the primitive hill tribes of the Madhya Pradesh. From
the point of view of the New England congregation,
its representatives who pushed over the Mississipi
were just as much missionaries as those who went to
China. So the Tamil congregation in South India is
scarcely less remote from the Gonds of the Madhya
Pradesh than it is from the Papuans of New Guinea.
Those who go out from there to either service are
missionaries.

One further reservation needs to be made with
regard to the word 'abroad'. Within the geographical
neighbourhood of a Christian community there may
well be some area of need which calls for a direct
missionary approach, which is indisputably distinct
from the ordinary round of that community's parochial
life. For such service some individual or group of individuals will, after special training, be sent by the
Church. Such men and women will be missionaries in
the strictest sense of that term. They may not be
going overseas, but they will be going 'abroad' into a
world of new relationships and with a different intellectual climate from anything to which they have been
accustomed in their local church life. We are already
familiar with the idea of chaplains in industry, with

industrial missioners. In recent years much attention has been attracted to the work of the 'Mission de Paris' directed, as that has been, towards the largely pagan masses of industrial France. No body of men could better claim the title of missionaries than the devoted priests of that Mission and the no less devoted lay 'militants' who shared their Mission.

Yet when each of these reservations has been made and the fullest recognition given to the proper non-geographical sense in which it is legitimate to use the term missionary, there remains a distinctive sense in which that term applies to those who, in 'going abroad', do in fact go overseas on what is, from the point of view of those who send them and those who receive them, a 'foreign mission'. If we are, in any way, to describe 'how' Christians are to obey the divine imperative to-day it is of great consequence that we should understand the nature of the 'foreign mission' of the Church.

Our initial task is to establish the importance of the word 'foreign'[1] so that the fulfilment of its obedience, on the part of any local embodiment of the Church, shall be seen to involve a foreign missionary concern and activity.

The Christian Church is deeply committed to the conviction that in Christ, and nowhere else, God has reconciled the world to Himself. This does not mean

---

[1] This acceptance of the word 'foreign' is involved in any serious attempt to recognize the validity and value of differences which distinguish between but need not divide Christians. There is, of course, a way of being 'foreign' which is obnoxious.

that God has not in many and various ways revealed Himself to men. As Paul told the crowd at Lystra, God has not left Himself without witness[1] in any nation. But what the Church claims is that it is only in Christ that He is fully revealed as Saviour. That revelation is for all men everywhere. But how can they hear without a preacher? And how can they preach except they be sent? As long as there are any who do not know of what God has done in Christ, missionaries from foreign parts will, in fact, be needed if the divine imperative 'go preach' is to be obeyed. And that applies as surely to the imperative 'go teach'. The Gospel is not only the most wonderful story in the world, and so must be told. It is a way of life by which the truth of the story is verified in Christian experience, and for this it is necessary that there shall be those who will obey the command to teach 'all that I have commanded you'. The full content of what is involved in observing Christ's commands will, as Paul saw clearly, call for the widest and most generous sharing amongst Christians. Only 'with all the saints' will it be possible 'to comprehend . . . what is the breadth and length and height and depth, and to know the love of Christ which surpasses knowledge, that you may be filled with all the fulness of God.'[2]

Again, as we look out on a world deeply riven by the divisions of class and race, of nation and ideology, there is an inescapable imperative laid upon the Christian to go and heal. And this healing Mission is

[1] Acts 14. 17.
[2] Eph. 3. 18–19.

one which is most effective at the level where it is most personal. It is no accident that it was to an individual that Jesus told the story of the Samaritan traveller and what he did for a wounded Jew, and then said 'go and do thou likewise'. That story described a work of healing which far transcended the physical ministration of pouring in oil and wine and binding up the injured man. It set in train a process of thinking which made of the differences between races things which could be enjoyed instead of barriers which made for separation. If the Church is to obey the imperative 'go heal' it is involved in a foreign mission in every country in the world without exception. There can, in such a mission, be no 'sending' countries as distinct from 'receiving' countries. Every country is called to send. Every country needs to receive.

Yet again, if the Church is to succeed in demonstrating that the Gospel can touch the deep levels of a people's life, its language, its customs, its culture, so that a Christian society can emerge, then the contribution of the foreigner is necessary. The foreigner who can speak out of the experience of his own people's life and history and show how the influence of Christ has modified laws, moulded custom, inspired culture, is a living witness to the fact that what has happened in one place can happen elsewhere. This, as we have seen earlier, is one aspect of the meaning of obedience to the imperative 'go baptize'.

No Church can afford to be without the inspiration of a foreigner's obedience to the missionary imperative, just as no Church can itself be fully obedient to that imperative without being committed to a foreign mission.

With that understanding of the intrinsic importance of the 'foreign' element in the Mission of the Church, of 'going abroad' as one essential aspect of the obedience of the Church, we can now go on to consider the several forms under which this Mission is to be fulfilled to-day.

I would distinguish two main forms under which the missionary imperative is to be obeyed to-day, under each of which, though in different ways, that four-fold obedience we have been considering can be discharged. In making this distinction which is indispensable for clear thinking, there is a real problem of language to be overcome. If the Mission of the Church is a Mission of the Church as a whole, if the Christian imperative applies to all who understand and accept the call to Christian discipleship, then in a profound sense, as we have already seen, every Christian disciple is a missionary. Tradition and the accepted use of language, however, have determined that the word 'missionary' shall normally be confined to a particular 'calling'. It is the normal designation for the men and women who believe that they have received a definite 'call' to 'preach', 'teach', 'heal', 'baptize', and to this end they direct their lives. Others confirming this sense of mission undertake so to provide for their material needs that they will be relieved of anxiety and preoccupation on that score and be free to follow their 'calling', to be available for all such service of the

Mission of the Church as calls for the maximum of undistracted attention. That is the traditional understanding of the word missionary.

Meanwhile to-day all those who are at all aware of the expanding horizons of the missionary task are quite clear that that task can never be seen in its true proportions if it is confined to the traditional understanding, either of the word Mission, or of the word missionary. Dr. Oldham has a searching passage which is relevant to our discussion. He writes—

'The need to restore the broken connection between the Church and life as it is actually lived demands a radically new understanding of the place and function of the lay members of the Church. There is a great deal of talk in church circles at the present time about the importance of the laity. But the question is approached almost invariably from the wrong end. What is usually meant is that more laymen should come in and give their support to the Church as it is. That is just what a large number of the best lay people at present standing on the fringe will not do. The much more important question to which the Church needs to address its mind is its own need of the experience which these people have of life to widen its outlook and deepen its understanding, so that it may become a more effective force in society. If Christianity is not something existing apart from life but is the transfiguration of life itself— and that means in the end the transfiguration of the whole of life—it is those who are in the front line of the battle and are exposed to the severest tests who can best teach us what Christianity means as a living faith. It is through its lay members that the Church makes contact with the life of the world.'[1]

[1] J. H. Oldham, op. cit., p. 89.

The discerning reader will recognize in those last two sentences that Dr. Oldham has, in other words, given a definition of our four-fold imperative as it can be obeyed, and often is being obeyed, by those to whom the word missionary in its usual sense would never be applied. The Christian men and women who 'go abroad' in the service of their particular country, who go as agents of commerce, who play their part in welfare services and development schemes, are clearly a vital part of the Christian Mission. It is they who, in the actual work-a-day life of the world, in a society increasingly dominated by a secular view of life, have to make Christianity visible, who, to quote Dr. Oldham again, have 'to show that it is a possible way of looking at things'.[1] In doing this they are interpreters, teachers, healers. In the sense in which we have seen that it is legitimate to use the word, they 'baptize'. It is, however, very much to be doubted if they would welcome the title of 'missionary' even if it were offered to them, though they would often readily acknowledge that they went to their work with a genuine sense of Mission. The problem of nomenclature remains. Perhaps in the very nature of things it is insoluble. Perhaps, indeed, what happened at Antioch long ago is the real answer. We are told in the Acts that 'in Antioch the disciples were for the first time called Christians'.[2] If, by the way men and women live in business and professional life, in public service and in the circle of the home, others recognize that they are,

[1] J. H. Oldham, op. cit., p. 10.
[2] Acts 11. 26.

in fact, following Christ then the Mission is indeed being fulfilled at a fundamental level. Yet it was these very Christians, busy in the market places of Antioch, in its civic and industrial life, who recognized that for the fulfilment of the Mission in all its ranges some must be 'set apart' for a different kind of service.[1]

The most important thing about which we have to be clear is that in distinguishing between different kinds of service we are never for one moment making judgments of value. Value is given by God's call, and by nothing else, and if His call is to service on the frontiers of the 'lay' world, then for the man or woman so called there can be no higher vocation. 'Now there are varieties of gifts', writes Paul, 'but the same Spirit; and there are varieties of service, but the same Lord; and there are varieties of working, but it is the same God who inspires them all in every one. To each is given the manifestation of the Spirit for the common good.'[2]

Being clear then that there is no distinction of value between the 'callings' of God, and repudiating the superficial difference between 'whole time' and 'part time' service as a radically false estimate of the varieties of the divine working, we can attempt to understand what are the particular characteristics and responsibilities of the foreign missionary vocation, as traditionally defined, and what are those of the 'lay' apostolate 'abroad'.

[1] Acts 13. 2.
[2] I Cor. 12. 4–7.

First then we have to understand the nature of the calling of the foreign missionary. So much has been said and written in recent years about the necessity that he shall be the servant of the Church in which he finds himself that perhaps we may take that truth as needing no additional argument or proof. In no way conflicting with that truth, but even more fundamental, is the fact that he has a calling from God. Surprising as it may seem, and perhaps a little disconcerting to all concerned, part of his vocation is to be 'foreign'. Indeed only in so far as his 'foreignness' is not only recognized but welcomed can he, in fact, be of that service to the Church for which God has called him. All that we have already considered of the importance of the 'foreign' element in the life of any and every Church is involved here.

This means that, whatever be the particular form of service assigned to him by the Church he serves, he has two distinctive characteristics. In the first place he is there to represent something which without his presence would not be represented. He represents the on-going life of obedience of another Christian community. He is a living testimony to another experience. He is a witness to a fellowship in the gospel which is universal. It is almost impossible to exaggerate the importance of this aspect of the foreign missionary, at a moment in history when the separating bitterness of nationalism is threatening the Church at that point where its witness to the world is perhaps more needed than anywhere else.

In the second place he is an interpreter. As such he

has a dual role to perform. On the one hand he has the insights of the community from which he comes as to the ways in which the missionary imperative can best be obeyed. These he has to interpret to the Church in which he serves. But that Church itself is already active in its obedience to the same imperative. The foreign missionary is, therefore, also the interpreter of the devotion of the Church which receives him back to the Church which has sent him. He is the outward and visible symbol of that 'mutual dependence, mutual consideration and mutual helpfulness'[1] by which the Church on an international scale can obey the apostolic injunction 'Bear ye one another's burdens, and so fulfil the law of Christ.'[2]

In passing it may be noted that in some parts of the world during the short twilight of colonialism there are those who are being *recruited* by the Church to serve in certain specialist capacities, mostly in education, *at the charges* of the local government. Such men and women have a peculiarly difficult vocation to fulfil. As things are they are contracted for by the Church for a service with the State over which the Church has a steadily diminishing control. At the same time the State accepts only a limited liability for these men and women. Serving both Church and State they are wholly at the disposal of neither. This anomalous position is the accident of peculiar circumstances which can hardly be expected to endure. Meanwhile such men and women have an immensely

[1] J. H. Oldham, op. cit., p. 41.
[2] Gal. 6. 2.

[131]

important witness to give, are as certainly part of the Christian Mission as any of their fellows. They should be afforded the fullest possible service that the Church can offer them, not only in the land in which they serve, but also in the land from which they come.

There remains to be considered the nature of the calling of the Christian man or woman who goes 'abroad' in a 'lay' capacity. In this capacity he has been contracted for by a government or a business concern, or an agency, maybe international, whose purpose is some aspect of human welfare. Such a Christian has an essential duty to perform to his employers. They, for their part, accept certain liabilities for his support. The employer is serving his own ends, ends which may well be good in themselves and contributing to the divine purpose for mankind, but which are so incidentally and not essentially, at the most implicitly, never explicitly. In what sense, then, are we to understand the missionary vocation of the man or woman who goes abroad in such service?

There is, I suggest, a double sense in which men and women may be called by God to such service, and in their serving be obeying the missionary imperative, and be an essential part of the Mission of the Church. First, then, the place of their service is one of the frontiers of the Church's Mission. If our argument has been true, the whole of human life has to be claimed for God. His writ must be seen to run effectively through every aspect of human society. To acquiesce in anything less ambitious is, for the Christian, to surrender his central conviction that Christ is King of kings and Lord of lords. If that is recognized, then we can see a real sense in which the Christian on this frontier is a representative and an interpreter. To-day, perhaps, to a greater extent than in some previous periods he is in both capacities an explorer. He has to discover 'how' on that particular frontier what he represents can be effectively applied. Only after such exploration can he become an interpreter, 'baptizing' this new frontier in the name of Christ and helping the Church as a whole to understand the nature of the new territory for which it now has a new responsibility.

This difficult and delicate task of exploration is one which can only be undertaken by men and women who see this frontier of service as a place to which God has called them. In their obedience to this missionary calling they obey the missionary imperative as only they can obey it. Here is the 'lay' apostolate for which there can be no alternative provision other than the layman.

In the *second* place the layman who is fulfilling his missionary vocation on this frontier 'abroad' is interpreting to the men and women of that country, and to his fellow-churchmen there, 'how' the Christian imperative can be obeyed. And he is doing this not only at the domestic level or within the Christian community itself, but on the frontiers of the world which that local Christian community is called to redeem. He can only be such an interpreter because he himself is wholly involved on this frontier.

There, then, are the two distinctive forms under which the 'foreign' mission of the Church has to be recognized. In one sense it is true that there is nothing new about this. These distinctive 'obediences' have always been a feature of the life of the Church from the earliest days. But during recent centuries there has been a tendency to narrow the understanding of how the Christian imperative is to be obeyed. In our world to-day, in which so deliberate and sustained an attack is being made upon the validity of the Christian interpretation of God's ways with man, it is the more essential that we should see clearly the wide range of the Christian Mission, and how manifold are those 'varieties of service' through which the same Lord is working.

If we have understood the scope of the Mission correctly, have glimpsed how much is involved in these imperatives, it must surely be obvious that the man and woman who is to be sent 'abroad' in either capacity will need some special training. The Conference of the International Missionary Council, held at Willingen in Germany in 1952, gave much thought to what is involved in training for the Mission. In the findings of the Conference three qualities were described as being essential for the missionary—'sensitiveness, flexibility, alertness'. The vocation of the missionary was assumed, and his training in the faith he had to expound was carefully noted. But it was insisted that for the actual performance of his task these three qualities were indispensable.

The man or woman who goes 'abroad', whose 'foreignness' is part of the contribution he has to make, must be extremely sensitive to the people of the land in which he serves. Their ways and habits of thought are as foreign to him as his to theirs. They have a culture and a history of their own which help to explain them and their reactions to him and to everything he says and does. He has, in a word, to be a man with multiple antennæ capable of picking up the slightest radiations of thought and feeling which come from those with whom he is now associated.

Likewise it stands to reason that such a man in such an environment has to be flexible in outlook and attitude. If he is doctrinaire in his approach to situations, dogmatic in his attitude to people, he will fail as an interpreter, for he will not be listened to; and failing as an interpreter he will be discounted as a representative—or, what is more serious than his being so discounted, he will be responsible for mis-representation which, more than anything else, will spell the failure of a Mission.

Meanwhile, in addition to being a good learner, apt to receive and to do so gracefully, in addition to being capable of adjusting both himself and his ideas, he has to be a man alert to the real needs of the local situation, which real needs provide him with the opportunities for his Mission.

These three qualities are indispensable, under which-ever of the two forms of service a man or woman goes 'abroad' to obey the Christian imperative. And these qualities are the by-product of good training. No

Christian man or woman, whatever their professional qualifications, however wide their technical experience, ought to be allowed to go 'abroad' to-day without preliminary training for the Christian Mission. Scarcely less important is the necessity for facilities to be provided for their refreshment and reconditioning for further service during their periods of leave in their home country. Few things are more disconcerting in the present picture of the Christian Mission than the almost frivolous irresponsibility with which the authorities in many Churches and in some missionary agencies treat this vital matter of training Christians for service 'abroad'.

This, of course, is not to say that there is any one form of training which has to be received by all or could possibly be appropriate for all. What is called for is the far more vigorous support of existing provision, a steady increase in its range and a readiness to make experiments.

Here it is encouraging to observe that pioneers have already been at work, men and women who either inherited older traditions of such training and have begun to adapt them to the needs of a new day, or those who have explored entirely new ventures for which no precedents existed. As an illustration of the first, it is possible to cite Florence Allshorn in Britain whose life has been so vividly portrayed, her vision so faithfully interpreted, in a recent book by Dr. Oldham.[1] In one sense there was nothing original in

[1] *Florence Allshorn and the Story of St. Julian's,* by J. H. Oldham, 1951.

her insistence on reality in religion, but the way in which she interpreted this demand was creative in a new fashion. Such reality, she proved for herself and so was able to teach, depended on knowing oneself *with* others and not in isolation. If the word *with* was to have real content it meant facing one's own failings and the failings of others without either illusion or disillusion, and, again, it needed to be a mutual discovery. Above all *together* there had to be shared the belief that God calls to perfection. Where she saw more clearly than most was that this needs time and is not something that can be hurried. To this end she and others founded St. Julian's as a place and as a community in which 'sensitiveness, flexibility and alertness' could be pursued. In the process she has started a revolution in the approach to the training of the 'foreign missionary'.

Florence Allshorn built on older foundations. For all her originality which was profound, she had to hand something which could be adapted. She pioneered from within a missionary fellowship. Others, in our time, have had to break completely new ground. One illustration of this in America can be seen in the Meadville Conference for outgoing missionaries, an experiment barely two years old which is seeking to explore within the context of the United States how men and women going 'abroad' can *together* begin to see how important 'sensitiveness, flexibility, alertness' are for their Mission. Sponsored by the Foreign Missions Division of the National Council of the Churches of Christ of the United States this pioneering venture deserves the maximum of support as well as, we may hope, the maximum liberty for experiment, such as is surely called for in days when going 'abroad' as an American missionary is not the easiest of callings.

Yet another illustration of a centre where the 'how' of obedience to the Church's Mission is being most carefully studied is the Ecumenical Institute at Bossey, in Switzerland. Dr. Hendrik Kraemer, until this year its director, has sought to make it a place to which men and women drawn from many countries could come and study together the frontier condition of our time and see how in these conditions the missionary imperative has to be interpreted. Groups of men and women drawn from particular professions can meet here to study their own particular frontier problems. In some conferences the company will be much more widely constituted. In yet others the 'foreign missionary' will meet with those called to the 'lay' apostolate to discover how they belong together. And all this happens against the background of a community which gives a new and richer understanding of the meaning of Christian fellowship. Something of what Bossey represents as a centre of training for the Mission can be gleaned from words spoken by Dr. Kraemer at Evanston:

'This "home" character of the Ecumenical Institute', he said, 'is permanent, since even when there are no meetings in progress it is a home for all the resident staff, who have to be a community and to create an atmosphere of which everybody who pays a visit, be it short or long, is aware. In short, it has to be a sustaining and inspiring "home". Sustaining for those who live there permanently and for all who have taken part in its life at its meetings, and through correspondence. Inspiring, because the Church in its calling, its misery and grandeur, becomes visible, entreating men to live a life primarily centred on Christ, the common Lord and Saviour. For this reason, the Institute, sometimes consciously, sometimes unconsciously, is the birthplace of important personal decisions and of new initiatives in various countries. By this living together the word "ecumenical" can be made a living experience. The World Council of Churches has nowhere which embodies this continuously apart from the Ecumenical Institute.'

One more pioneer venture in training for the Mission is to be found in an experiment which has now been in progress in Britain for a little over a year. Known as *Oversea Service* this is the exploration of a virtually untouched field, at least as far as Britain is concerned. Government departments concerned with the recruitment of staff for overseas, business houses with large overseas connections are becoming increasingly aware that young men and women who go abroad to-day are urgently in need of guidance if, in addition to being professionally competent, they are to establish right relationships with the people of the country to which they go. Lack of 'sensitiveness, flexibility and alertness' on the part of its servants, can be as disastrous to a government and to a business house as to the Church. Beginning as an attempt to provide basic training for 'lay' service overseas, Christianly understood, this new venture sees opening up ahead of it the urgent need both for the effective linking up of those who go 'abroad' with the Church where they are to serve, as well as with others similarly 'trained' and for the creation of just such a 'home' base as is provided at Bossey. Sponsored by the British Council of Churches and the Conference of British Missionary Societies this experiment has already begun to demonstrate that it is meeting a real need.

All of these enterprises, and others which might have been mentioned, are deliberately concerned to prepare men and women for the new frontiers to which the Christian imperative has to be applied to-day. It is too early yet to say what enduring success will attend the particular experiments here described. But it is certainly possible to claim for those who have initiated them, and who are serving in them, that they themselves have been seized of the urgent necessity that, in the Christian Mission of our time, 'sensitiveness, flexibility and alertness' are necessary elements in the equipment for every man and woman who, under one form or another, has heard God's call to 'go preach', 'go teach', 'go heal', 'go baptize'. They are actual illustrations of the manner in which disciples to-day are beginning to learn the 'how' of obedience in a world from which so many traditional landmarks have been washed away. They are, indeed, each of them in their several ways, acts of faith in the Christian imperative, acts of loyalty to the One who said 'go' and who accompanies all those who obey Him. To the Spirit of that commitment these lectures have been an attempt to afford an introduction. We may perhaps sum up the whole matter in some words which Dr. Oldham has quoted in his book, *Life is Commitment*.

'There is only one place at which a genuine renewal of the life of the Church can take place, namely at the point at which its mission of transforming the world is being fulfilled. The only real renewal is a healing and saving manifestation of the power of love in open and courageous encounter with the world.'[1]

That place is the hill called Calvary, the mount of the Ascension, the place where we were baptized, the frontier where these three meet and become one.

[1] J. H. Oldham, op. cit., p. 91.

Index of Authors Quoted

A
Allshorn, Florence, 136, 137

B
Bailey, Sherwin, 105, 106

C
Carothers, J. C., 74, 75, 76, 78, 108

Cockin, F. A., Bishop of Bristol, 45, 46

Cook, Robert C., 79, 80

Cullmann, Oscar, 89, 94, 96, 97, 98

D
Dammers, A. H., 33, 54

Dix, Gregory, 35

F
Faris, 75

J
Jeffreys, M. V. C., 51, 52, 54, 58

K
Keats, John, 92

Kennedy, Studdert, 35

Kraemer, Kendrik, 138, 139

L
Lampe, G. W. H., 88, 89, 95

Lightfoot, J. B., 95

Lowry, Charles W., 90, 91

M
Maurice, F. D., 60, 61

Minear, Paul, 44, 45, 46

O
Oldham, J. H., 37, 118, 127, 128, 131, 136, 141

S
Sorley, Charles, 38

T
Tillich, Paul, 32

U
Underhill, Evelyn, 12

V
Vidler, A. R., 66

W
Wiles, Maurice, 35

Willoughby, W. C., 109

Index of Biblical References

MAX WARREN, D. D., was born in Dublin in 1904 and educated at Marlborough and Jesus College, Cambridge. After a year at Ridley Hall he went out as a layman under the Church Missionary Society to Northern Nigeria. On his return because of illness, he was ordained in the Winchester Diocese to a curacy at St. John's, Boscombe, England, with which he combined the joint secretaryship for Youth Work in the Diocese for the next four years. In 1936 he was appointed Vicar of Holy Trinity, Cambridge, and from there went to be General Secretary of the Church Missionary Society. In 1943 he received his Doctor's degree from Wycliffe College, Toronto.

Canon Warren has travelled widely throughout the world and has visited the United States many times. He attended the Second Assembly of the World Council of Churches at Evanston, Illinois, as a consultant.

He is the author of *Truth of Vision, The Triumph of God* and *The Christian Mission,* among other works.